SPIRITUAL LEADERSHIP TRANSFORMATION

Cultivating Inner Wisdom For Outer Influence

Vetri J Raman

Contents

Dedication

This book is dedicated to all the past, present, and future spiritual and leadership gurus of the world.

Your timeless wisdom, unwavering guidance, and inspiring examples light the path for countless individuals seeking to lead with integrity, compassion, and purpose. May your teachings continue to transform lives and empower leaders to create a better, more enlightened world.

Foreword to the Second Edition

As I sit down to write the foreword for the second edition of "Spiritual Leadership, "I am profoundly moved by the journey this book has taken since its initial release. The first edition marked a milestone in my life — my debut as an author. It was an ambitious project, one that aimed to delve deeply into the complex interplay of spirituality and leadership. While the feedback was overwhelmingly positive, it was also a mirror showing me where I could enhance my readers' understanding and engagement.

Many readers found the Indian cultural references and terms challenging, which sometimes made the core messages less accessible. Others pointed out the inherent difficulty of the subject matter itself, reflecting on their struggles to connect with the deeper introspective challenges posed by the book. Notably, senior leaders expressed that the book's call for self-criticism was both necessary and tough, aligning precisely with my intention — to encourage leaders to reflect deeply on their actions and beliefs.

Amidst these reflections, some readers contacted me after reading the stories, feeling like they saw their own experiences in them. I always replied the same way: "If you think it's your story, then it is. If you don't, then it's not." What matters most is what you learn from the stories, not who they are about.

Taking all this into account, I was driven to revisit and refine my work. More than three years have passed since the first edition, and in that time, not only has my understanding deepened, but so has the reservoir of stories and insights I wish to share. This second edition is enriched with these additional narratives and an improved presentation to facilitate a better grasp of the spiritual dimensions of leadership.

The core purpose of this book remains unchanged. I am committed to helping leaders embark on a path of spiritual and moral introspection, which is crucial for genuine transformation. My goal was not to achieve overnight change but to plant seeds of contemplation that would gradually bear fruit in the minds and actions of those who lead.

I updated the title from "Spiritual Leadership" to "Spiritual Leadership Transformation" to better reflect our focus on transforming leadership behaviors and habits.

I invite you to explore this second edition with renewed clarity and focus. Whether you are revisiting or encountering these concepts for the first time, I hope that "Spiritual Leadership Transformation" will guide you toward profound personal and professional growth.

Introduction

Being a Leader is being Spiritual each day!!

Mahatma Gandhi, a visionary leader who guided millions through nonviolent resistance, exemplified leadership deeply anchored in spirituality. Facing enormous challenges, he relied on daily meditation and inner faith to draw strength, inspiring others to pursue truth and justice through peaceful methods. Data indicates that leaders who integrate spirituality into their practices experience a 23% boost in employee engagement and productivity. Being a leader is being spiritual each day, as it involves guiding others with compassion, integrity, and a deep sense of purpose.

Leadership has been a key topic for scholars for thousands of years, with experts providing insights since ancient times. Today, a quick online search about "leadership coaching" or "the differences between a leader and a manager" shows many resources available.

There are plenty of books, academic papers, and expert opinions, along with numerous consultants and coaches ready to improve leadership skills.

Despite ongoing focus on the importance of leadership in businesses and continued discussions by scholars over the years, real improvements in leadership skills are still hard to find.

With more than twenty years of experience as a leader and observer, I've observed a major gap in contemporary leadership. Many current leaders often miss essential soft skills and lack awareness of emotional dynamics, key elements of traditional leadership principles that they may overlook or undervalue.

My Motivation:

At one of the operational excellence conferences, I connected with a gentleman named Mike, who serves as an Operational Excellence Vice President at a multinational company. We discussed our respective organizational cultures and the role of leadership in shaping and managing these cultures.

Mike shared stories about the leadership challenges in his organization and why things were not as they should be. I also shared my own leadership experiences. We both agreed that the root cause of cultural problems often starts at the leadership level.

As we exchanged our respective stories, we realized that we had heard these stories before. It turned out that we had met at the same conference almost five years ago. This realization amused us, and we joked about how our stories hadn't changed.

Reflecting on my conversation with Mike after returning from the conference, I was struck by the fact that neither his organization nor mine had changed in the past five years.

Despite attending numerous conferences and investing heavily in leadership development and training, we found ourselves having the same critical conversations. This made me question how effective these efforts were in truly changing organizational culture.

I realized that we were fundamentally approaching the problem incorrectly. Leaders need to reflect on and change their own behaviors and habits before expecting their teams to follow suit. True cultural change starts with individual transformation.

Typically, when discussing the traits of a leader, we often hear terms like visionary, effective communicator, motivator, strategic thinker etc etc. These terms usually emphasize the individual's hard skills, while the softer, internal skills receive much less attention.

This observation inspired me to write this book. My goal is to highlight and raise awareness of the often-overlooked characteristics and skills that many of today's leaders either lack or struggle to comprehend and apply.

The purpose of the book is to act as a mirror for you, encouraging self-reflection and personal growth. It doesn't provide direct solutions to your problems but aims to help you discover your own solutions. The answers to our challenges lie within us; we just need to delve deeper to uncover them.

In ancient Indian philosophy, the term "Swadharma" signifies one's personal duty or righteous path, which is uniquely determined by an individual's inherent nature, roles, and responsibilities in life. Derived from "swa" (own) and "dharma" (duty/righteousness), it underscores the concept that each person has a distinct set of duties and moral obligations that align with their personal nature, abilities, and social context.

This concept prioritizes gaining a deeper knowledge of oneself before attempting to comprehend the situations of family members or colleagues. Additionally, effective leadership is seen as beginning with self-awareness; leaders are encouraged to first understand themselves before trying to understand their team.

This philosophy identifies four main goals of life, known as Purushartha, a term in Sanskrit (one of the oldest languages in the world) that translates to "purpose of life."

The four objectives of human existence are:

Artha (Wealth or Prosperity): This involves the generation of wealth to escape poverty and contribute positively to society, typically resulting in happiness and pleasure.

Kama (Pleasure or desire) is the quest for enjoyment via the five senses—sight, hearing, taste, smell, and touch—and includes both mental and sensual gratifications. It emphasizes ethically experiencing pleasure.

Dharma (Duty or Righteousness): This entails striving to comprehend the human condition, addressing problems, and discovering one's true course of moral integrity. It is associated with the responsibility to maintain social norms and helps to guide the pursuits of both artha and kama.

Moksha (Liberation or Enlightenment): The ultimate goal, which is achieving freedom from worldly desires. It signifies the cessation of illusions and achieving self-satisfaction, self-realization, and self-love.

Let us dive a bit :

Artha: The Story of Samaira, the Social Entrepreneur

Samaira was once a young financial analyst, skilled and ambitious, who recognized the glaring inequalities in her bustling city. Her desire for wealth was not merely for personal gain but was rooted in a vision to uplift the impoverished communities that lay in the stark shadows of skyscrapers. She ventured into social entrepreneurship, launching a start-up that used innovative technology to provide affordable housing solutions. As her company flourished, not only did she create substantial wealth, but she also contributed significantly to society, bringing joy and stability to thousands of lives. Her journey highlighted how Artha, when aligned with ethical intentions, leads to societal benefit and personal happiness.

Kama: The Journey of Leo the Chef

Leo was a celebrated chef whose life revolved around the art of culinary pleasures. He believed in the sanctity of the five senses and dedicated his career to creating experiences that delighted them. His restaurant was a haven where every dish served was an ode to Kama—celebrating not just taste but the ambiance, the music, and the very act of dining as a joyful, communal experience. Leo's mastery in crafting such experiences taught him and his patrons the importance of enjoying life's pleasures, yet always through legitimate and respectful means, thus enriching his life and those around him.

Dharma: The Resolve of Aisha the Lawyer

Aisha, a determined lawyer, worked tirelessly to bring justice to those who felt powerless. Her career was her calling, and through it, she sought to understand deeper human conditions and societal issues. With each case, Aisha stood firm in her values of honesty and integrity, often being a pillar for those who had no one else to champion their cause. Her dedication not only brought resolution to many conflicts but also upheld and reinforced societal values, showing that Dharma involves living one's truth while contributing positively to the community.

Moksha: The Enlightenment of Guru Devan

Guru Devan spent his life in pursuit of spiritual wisdom, traveling far from the material comforts of his youth to understand the deeper meanings of existence. His journey was marked by meditation, teaching, and moments of profound enlightenment. Over the years, Devan realized that true liberation came from letting go of earthly desires and embracing a love for the self that transcended material needs. His teachings inspired many to seek Moksha, illustrating that the ultimate freedom comes from within and manifests as peace and fulfillment beyond the physical realm.

Each of these stories from both the spiritual world and modern leadership illustrates the timeless relevance of the four goals of human life, showing how they can be integrated into various aspects of personal and professional endeavors for a balanced and fulfilling life.

Let us go through this once again to get a better clarity on the goals of human life.

Artha: The Tale of Nina the Tech Innovator

Nina, a visionary in the tech industry, saw an opportunity to bridge the digital divide that plagued underdeveloped regions around her. Driven by the principle of Artha, she founded a company dedicated to creating affordable, easy-to-use tech solutions that would enable remote education and healthcare access. Her innovations not only accumulated wealth for her and her stakeholders but also significantly improved the quality of life for millions, demonstrating that the pursuit of wealth, when aligned with the common good, can generate widespread happiness and societal advancement.

Kama: The Story of Elena the Music Therapist

Elena, a talented musician with a deep understanding of the healing properties of sound, dedicated her life to music therapy. She used her skills to tap into the essence of Kama by enriching the lives of her clients through sound, helping them to recover from trauma and mental health issues. Her therapy sessions were a symphony of healing, showcasing the power of legitimate pleasure through the auditory senses. Elena's work not only brought joy to her clients but also fulfilled her own desire for a meaningful and pleasurable life.

Dharma: The Commitment of James the Environmentalist

James, an environmental scientist, committed his life to preserving the planet's biodiversity. Understanding that Dharma involves maintaining the balance of nature, he spearheaded global initiatives to combat deforestation and climate change. His actions, grounded in sincerity and a deep respect for ecological balance, inspired communities worldwide to adopt sustainable practices. James's dedication proved that true Dharma involves not just understanding human needs but also ensuring the health and longevity of the environment we depend on.

Moksha: The Path of Sanya, the Meditation Guru

Sanya, after years in the corporate grind, turned to meditation to find solace and meaning beyond material success. She became a meditation guru, teaching others the path to inner peace and liberation from material desires. Her teachings focused on self-awareness and mindfulness as tools for achieving Moksha. Sanya's journey and guidance illuminated the paths of many seeking tranquility and detachment in a chaotic world, offering a modern interpretation of achieving personal enlightenment and self-contentment.

These alternative stories still embody the essence of the four life goals but introduce new characters and settings, illustrating the universal application and adaptability of these ancient concepts in contemporary contexts.

Unraveling Misconceptions: "What Spirituality Is Not"

Often, gaining a clear understanding of something involves recognizing what it isn't.

Spirituality often emerges as a central theme in the modern quest for meaning and purpose. Yet, despite its rising popularity, its essence is frequently clouded by misconceptions and misinterpretations. To truly embrace its potential, it is essential to clarify what spirituality is not.

1. **Spirituality is Not Necessarily Religious**

One common misconception is that spirituality and religion are synonymous. While spirituality can be part of religious practice, it transcends organized faiths and doctrines. It is a broader search for a deeper understanding of life, a connection to something greater than oneself that does not automatically require adherence to the rituals and beliefs of a specific religion. Spirituality is about personal growth and understanding, which can happen both within and outside religious contexts.

2. **Spirituality is Not a Quick Fix for Life's Problems**

Another misunderstanding is viewing spirituality as a quick fix or an escape hatch from the challenges of daily life. Unlike some commercialized versions of spiritual practices that promise instant peace and enlightenment, true spirituality is a journey. It involves deep introspection, continuous learning, and personal development. It is not about avoiding problems but about fostering inner strength and perspective to deal with them more effectively.

3. **Spirituality is Not About Outward Appearances**

In the age of social media, it's easy to equate spirituality with aesthetic symbols like crystals, incense, or exotic retreats. However, true spirituality is an internal process. It's about how you feel, think, and connect with the world, not about external tools or appearances. While these elements might enhance one's spiritual exploration, they do not define spirituality itself.

4. **Spirituality is Not Exclusive or Elitist**

Spirituality is universally accessible. It is not reserved for a select few who have reached a certain level of enlightenment or those who have withdrawn from society to live ascetic lives. Everyone possesses the potential to explore their spiritual dimension, regardless of their social, economic, or cultural background. It's about finding meaning and connection in one's own life and is as individual and unique as each person.

5. **Spirituality is Not Passive**

There's a notion that being spiritual means being passively peaceful or detached from the world's problems. On the contrary, many spiritual traditions encourage active engagement with the world through acts of kindness, social justice, and community involvement. Spirituality can involve robust action aligned with personal values and compassion for others. It's not about withdrawing from the world but engaging with it authentically and purposefully.

Dispelling these myths about spirituality can open doors to a more genuine and fulfilling spiritual practice. It can help individuals connect with the true essence of spirituality, which is a deeply personal, transformative journey that varies from one individual to another. By understanding what spirituality is not, we can better understand what it can be—a path to profound personal change and a deeper understanding of life itself.

Spirituality and Its Link to Pain and Pleasure

Spirituality often explores the intricate balance between pain and pleasure, teaching that both are essential components of the human experience. Here, we examine how this relationship is understood through a story from ancient spiritual traditions and a modern leadership narrative.

The Tale of Sushila and the Lotus Flower

Sushila, an elderly and wise sage, lived by a serene lake filled with lotuses. Her teachings drew many who sought enlightenment. One day, a troubled young seeker named Arav came to her, overwhelmed by life's suffering. He saw no purpose in pain and questioned the existence of a compassionate universe.

Sushila led Arav to the edge of the water and pointed to a lotus flower, explaining, "Notice how the lotus, despite growing in muddy and unpleasant conditions, blossoms beautifully. It does not resist the mud, nor does it rush to bloom in comfort. Both the mud (pain) and the water (pleasure) are crucial for its growth."

Sushila continued, "In life, pain and pleasure are not opposites but complements. Pain pushes us to grow, to reevaluate our paths, and to strengthen our spirits, much like the mud for the lotus. Pleasure, meanwhile, offers respite and reward, nurturing our growth. Embracing both with acceptance and balance is key to spiritual awakening."

Arav spent many days contemplating this by the lake, slowly learning to accept life's pains as opportunities for growth and its pleasures as moments of gratitude. This transformative understanding led him towards a profound inner peace.

The Story of Sr Executive Maya

Maya, a successful executive of a leading manufacturing organization, faced significant challenges during the covid period. The pressure to lay off employees was immense, and the looming pain of tough decisions quickly overshadowed the pleasure of previous successes.

Instead of succumbing to despair, Maya saw this as a spiritual challenge. She held town hall meetings, openly discussing the company's challenges and her struggles with the decisions at hand. Her transparency and vulnerability turned the crisis into a collective journey, not just a corporate setback.

Maya implemented creative solutions that involved minimal layoffs, such as voluntary part-time work and temporary pay cuts, which were met with surprising support from the employees. Her leadership not only navigated the company through tough times but also deepened the collective spirit and loyalty of her team.

This experience taught Maya and her company that pain, while unpleasant, could lead to innovative solutions and tighter community bonds, while the pleasures of success, when shared, could build a resilient and dedicated workforce.

Both stories, one ancient and one modern, illustrate the profound spiritual truth that pain and pleasure are interconnected forces that shape our journey. In spirituality, as in leadership, the acceptance and balance of these experiences forge paths of growth, understanding, and ultimate fulfillment. Through these narratives, we see that embracing both the mud and the water, like the lotus, allows us to rise and bloom magnificently in the broad lake of life.

A Different Perspective on Spirituality

Think about the idea of helping others selflessly without expecting anything in return.

This narrative involves a woman and an poor young boy. One day, the boy came to the woman's door seeking financial assistance. Despite her own financial struggles, the woman noticed the boy was hungry and thirsty and offered him a glass of milk before sending him on his way.

As time went on, the woman aged and fell ill, necessitating surgery which led to a hospital stay. Upon discharge, she worried about her inability to settle the hefty medical bill. To her astonishment, she discovered that the bill had been cleared. Attached was a note expressing gratitude for the glass of milk—it was from the doctor who had operated on her, the same boy she had helped years ago.

This story exemplifies how acts of kindness, performed without expecting anything in return, can lead to profound reciprocation and increase our own joy manifold. It emphasizes that spreading joy not only enriches others but also enhances our own lives, much like Mother Teresa's example, who brought happiness to countless lives without expecting anything back.

Reflect on this: When considering the two interpretations of spirituality mentioned, how might this relate to leadership? Leadership is fundamentally about assisting others in areas like knowledge, skills, development, and personal ambitions, without seeking personal gain.

While leaders naturally expect their teams to strive towards organizational goals and fulfill their job responsibilities, true leadership involves fostering growth without any personal expectations in return.

The Spiritual Leadership Framework

Over my two decades of diverse professional experience, spanning both individual contributions and leadership positions. I've identified eight key aspects that define what I call "spiritual leadership elements". These elements, often overlooked in daily business operations, are crucial for both personal and professional growth.

To enhance clarity and visualization, I've arranged them into a structured framework. Using the familiar analogy of a business system, I've created a model to effectively illustrate these essential leadership qualities in a more vivid and relatable manner.

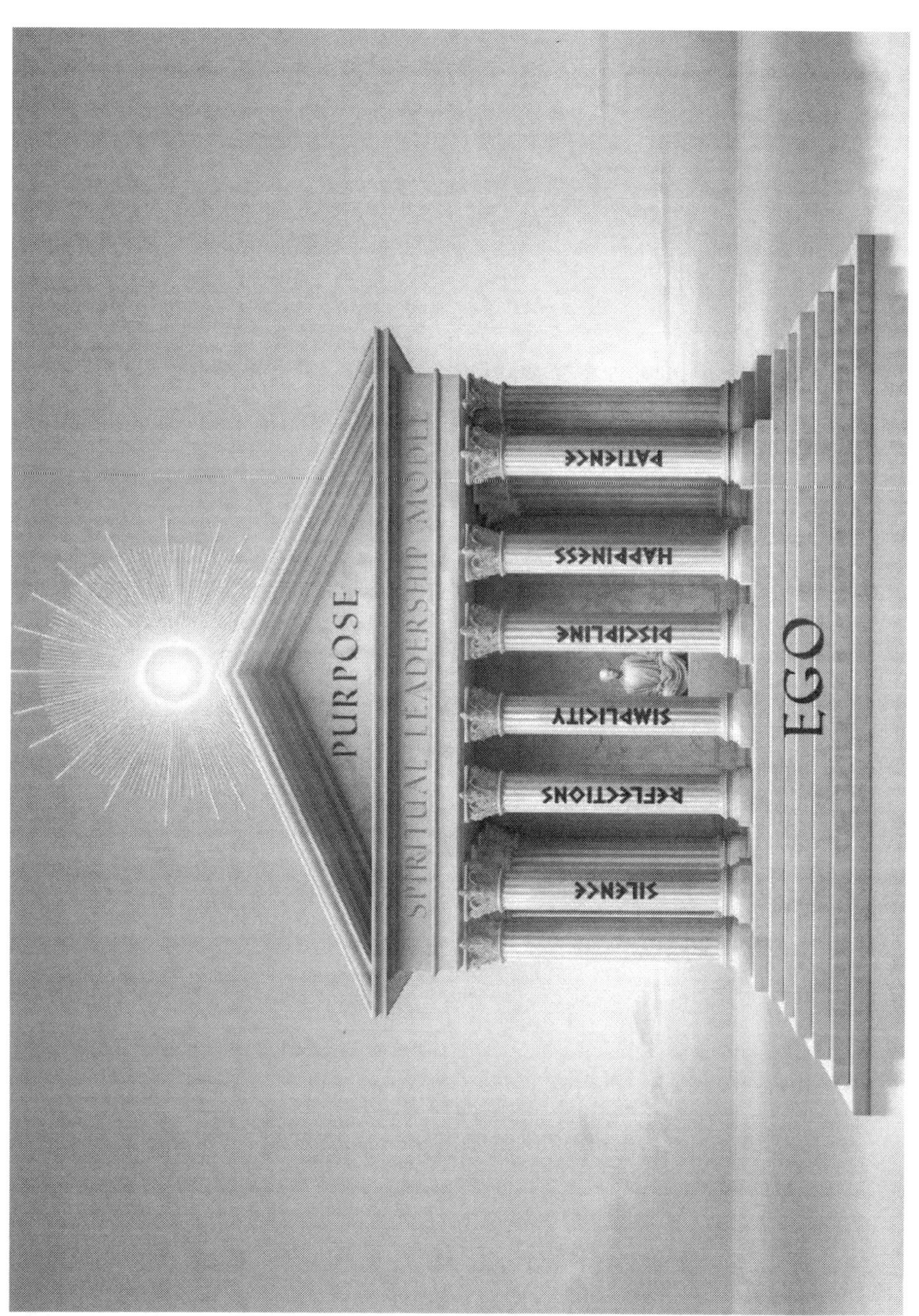
PURPOSE
SPIRITUAL LEADERSHIP MODEL
SILENCE
REFLECTIONS
SIMPLICITY
DISCIPLINE
HAPPINESS
PATIENCE
EGO

Leadership's Hidden Foundation: Ego and Humility

In the records of ancient spiritual traditions, the foundation of a grand temple was regarded as the cornerstone of its sacred strength. Hidden from sight, buried deep within the earth, this foundation was considered the most vital element of the temple's structure. Similarly, in our modern world, the foundation of a house, often unseen, plays a crucial role in its stability and longevity. Just as the roots of a mighty tree dig deep into the soil, anchoring it firmly and ensuring its survival through storms and seasons, the foundation of a house is indispensable for its endurance.

The Three anchors of Stability

Support and Stability: The foundation is the bedrock that supports the entire structure, ensuring it stands tall and unyielding.

Protection from the Elements: It shields the structure from environmental challenges such as snow, rain, wind, heat, noise, and fire.

Moisture shield: It prevents ground moisture from infiltrating the building, preserving its integrity and longevity.

Drawing a parallel to leadership, the unseen yet critical foundation of effective leadership is built on ego and humility. Just as the foundation of a house ensures its stability, the balance between ego and humility ensures the strength and resilience of leadership.

Ego: While often perceived negatively, a healthy ego is essential for confidence and assertiveness in leadership. It provides the drive and determination to lead effectively.

Humility: Balancing ego with humility is vital. Humility allows a leader to be selfless, acknowledging the contributions of others and remaining open to feedback and growth.

The Modern Leader's Path

In the fast-paced and ever-changing landscape of modern leadership, the foundational elements of ego and humility play three key roles:

Exhibiting Selflessness: True leadership is about putting the needs of the team and organization above personal ambitions.

Managing Ego: A leader must remain mentally stable and composed, even under intense external pressures.

Controlling Mood and Thoughts: Maintaining a positive and focused mindset is crucial for navigating the challenges of leadership.

Just as the ancient temple stood the test of time through its solid foundation, modern leaders must cultivate a balanced foundation of ego and humility. By doing so, they can lead with integrity, strength, and resilience, inspiring those around them and weathering the storms of change with grace and stability.

The Pillars of Leadership: Bridging Ancient Wisdom and Modern Strength

In the mystical tales of ancient spiritual traditions, the pillars of grand temples were revered not just for their physical support, but for their symbolic significance. These pillars, often intricately carved and adorned, stood as embodiments of strength and beauty, bearing the weight of the roof and transferring the immense load to the steadfast foundation below. Their role was both structural and aesthetic, enhancing the temple's grandeur while ensuring its stability.

The Pillars of Leadership

Just as these ancient pillars upheld the sanctity and splendor of temples, modern leadership is sustained by essential pillars that provide both strength and grace.

These pillars in leadership are patience, silence, discipline, simplicity, happiness, and self-reflection. Each of these qualities contributes to the spiritual and emotional fortitude of a leader, ensuring their resilience and stability.

Patience: The ability to endure and remain calm under pressure, allowing time for thoughtful decision-making.

Silence: Embracing moments of quiet reflection to gain clarity and insight, listening more than speaking.

Discipline: Maintaining focus and dedication to goals and principles, fostering a sense of responsibility and reliability.

Simplicity: Striving for simplicity in actions and thoughts, cutting through complexity to find clear, effective solutions.

Happiness: Cultivating a positive and joyful outlook, inspiring and motivating others.

Self-Reflection: Regularly assessing one's actions and motivations, promoting continuous personal growth and self-awareness.

The Modern Leader's Pillars

In the realm of contemporary leadership, these six pillars serve as the bedrock of a leader's character and effectiveness. By understanding and developing these qualities, leaders can navigate the complexities of their roles with greater ease and resilience.

Patience: Just as a pillar stands firm through the ages, a patient leader withstands challenges, making measured decisions that lead to long-term success.

Silence: In the quiet moments, a leader finds wisdom and perspective, akin to the silent strength of a temple pillar.

Discipline: The disciplined leader, like the unyielding pillar, upholds their commitments and sets a standard for others.

Simplicity: By embracing simplicity, leaders create clarity and focus, much like the straightforward elegance of a well-crafted pillar.

Happiness: A leader who fosters happiness spreads positivity, building a supportive and motivated team.

Self-Reflection: Continuous self-reflection ensures that a leader remains grounded and true to their values, strengthening their leadership foundation.

Just as the ancient pillars provided indispensable support to sacred structures, these six qualities are vital for the modern leader. They create a robust framework that enhances both the strength and beauty of leadership, enabling leaders to bear the weight of their responsibilities with grace and stability. Through the integration of these timeless principles, leaders can inspire and lead with enduring strength and wisdom.

The Roof of Leadership: Ancient Spiritual Insights and Modern Purpose

In the sacred stories of ancient spiritual traditions, the roof of a grand temple was not merely a structural necessity but a symbol of divine protection and purpose. This final architectural element safeguarded the temple from the ravages of nature—snow, rain, fire, wind, and noise—while ensuring the safety, security, privacy, and insulation of the sanctified space within.

The Roof's Protective Embrace

Much like these ancient roofs, which shielded the spiritual havens from external threats, the modern concept of leadership has its own protective element: purpose. Purpose is the overarching vision that guides and guards an organization, providing direction and meaning to every endeavor.

The Leadership compass: Purpose

In leadership, purpose serves as the roof that shelters and strengthens the organization. It encompasses a leader's clear understanding of their fundamental reason for being, both in their specific role and within the broader organizational context. This purpose is crucial for protecting and nurturing the organization's workforce, ensuring their alignment with the collective vision and goals.

Alignment with Vision: Just as a roof aligns with the walls and foundation, a leader must align with the organization's vision, ensuring every action supports the overarching mission.

Translation of Vision: The purpose must be communicated effectively and translated into actionable language that resonates at all levels of the organization.

Commitment to Team Goals: A purposeful leader is dedicated to helping team members achieve their goals, fostering an environment where everyone feels valued and supported.

The Modern Leader's Protective Purpose

A leader's purpose acts as the protective roof, offering several essential benefits:

Safety and Security: By providing clear direction and stability, a leader ensures that the team feels secure and confident in their roles.

Privacy and Insulation: Purpose-driven leadership protects the team from external distractions and negative influences, allowing them to focus on their goals.

Inspiration and Motivation: A well-defined purpose inspires and motivates team members, fostering a sense of belonging and commitment to the organization's vision.

In the same way that the ancient roof safeguarded the sacred space, a leader's purpose protects and nurtures the organizational environment. By maintaining a clear and compelling purpose, leaders can guide their teams through challenges, ensuring the long-term success and harmony of the organization.

Through the wisdom of ancient spiritual insights and the application of modern leadership principles, the purpose becomes the roof that shelters and strengthens the entire structure, enabling it to stand resilient and united against the storms of the world.

While the foundation is frequently emphasized as the most vital component, the pillars and the roof are equally crucial in ensuring the structure's stability, safety, and durability. In this assembly, the roof, pillars, and foundation function collaboratively, each element playing a distinct role in safeguarding and sustaining those within.

Therefore, all eight elements of the spiritual leadership model are essential. They work together in harmony to deepen leadership insight and strengthen leadership skills, bridging the timeless wisdom of the spiritual realm with the demands of modern leadership.

Purpose

When the Why is clear, the how becomes easier

The Purpose of Life

Explore different beliefs about the purpose of life, each offering insights into our spiritual existence.

Some believe the purpose of life is to understand reality to lessen suffering. By living ethically, improving our minds, and seeking wisdom, we try to escape suffering.

In the village of Elmswood, lived an old philosopher named Elias, known for his wisdom. One autumn morning, a young girl named Mia asked him about his books. Elias invited her to sit by the river and share his thoughts on life.

He explained, "These books unlock the profound secrets of life and offer insights into easing our suffering. They teach that by living with integrity and constantly seeking wisdom; we can transcend the difficulties we face and find true serenity. Embracing these principles, we not only navigate through life's challenges but also rise above them, achieving a state of inner peace and fulfillment."

Elias picked up a leaf and said, "Like this leaf, we endure seasons and storms, but each cycle offers growth and beauty. We too must grow and seek wisdom to better ourselves and the world."

Inspired, Mia began her journey of understanding, embracing the wisdom Elias had shared. As the river flowed silently, Elias's teachings took root in Mia's heart, ready to be passed on to others.

Others think our purpose is to honor and deeply connect with a higher power. Following divine rules, sharing our beliefs, and aiming for a heavenly afterlife guide us toward spiritual satisfaction.

In a serene village nestled between rolling hills lived a humble shepherd named Thomas. Thomas believed that life's true purpose was to honor and connect deeply with a higher power. Every morning, he would climb to the highest hill to pray, seeking guidance and strength.

One evening, Thomas encountered a lost traveler named Anna, weary and seeking direction. Thomas shared his food and offered her a place to rest. As they sat by the fire, he spoke of his faith and how following divine rules and sharing his beliefs brought him peace and purpose.

Moved by Thomas's profound devotion, Anna asked how she could achieve similar spiritual fulfillment. Thomas responded, "Seek a deep connection with the higher power through prayer and acts of kindness. Live by divine principles and aspire to a heavenly afterlife. This journey will lead you to true and lasting fulfillment."

Inspired, Anna decided to embrace this spiritual journey. As she left the village, she felt a newfound sense of purpose, guided by the principles Thomas had shared. Their encounter marked the beginning of her spiritual awakening, during which she honored a higher power and strived for a heavenly afterlife.

Some view life as a test, where devotion to a supreme being guides us. Through strong commitment, we aim to gain favor and secure a place in paradise.

In a quiet, ancient town lived a devout woman named Miriam, known for her unwavering faith in a supreme being. She believed life was a divine test, and her every action was guided by her desire to pass it. Miriam spent her days in prayer, helping neighbors, and living by sacred teachings, her heart set on securing a place in paradise.

One stormy night, a weary traveler named Jacob knocked on her door, seeking refuge. Miriam welcomed him warmly, offering food and shelter. As they sat by the fire, she shared her beliefs with a passion that burned brighter than the flames.

"Life is a divine test," Miriam declared, her eyes ablaze with an unyielding passion. "Our devotion and actions are the measures by which our place in paradise is determined. Each good deed we perform, and every heartfelt prayer we offer is a step closer to earning divine favor. Imagine our lives as a mosaic, where every act of kindness and moment of genuine faith adds a vibrant piece. The more we contribute these pieces, the more beautiful and complete our journey becomes. By embracing this path of righteousness and unwavering faith, we not only secure our place in the afterlife but also bring light to the lives of those around us, creating a legacy of hope and spiritual fulfillment."

Jacob, deeply moved by her conviction, felt a stirring in his soul. He had wandered, but Miriam's words resonated with a truth he could no longer ignore. Inspired by her unwavering faith, he vowed to live a life of strong commitment, hoping to gain favor and secure his place in paradise.

As Jacob left Miriam's home, the storm had passed, and a serene dawn broke over the town. He felt a renewed sense of purpose, carrying Miriam's wisdom with him, determined to honor the supreme being and pass life's ultimate test.

Consider life as a balanced interaction with mysterious universal forces. Aligning with nature's rhythms, we seek balance and embrace the flow of cosmic energy.

In a remote village surrounded by towering mountains and lush forests, a wise elder named Aiko lived. She believed life was a balanced interaction with mysterious universal forces. Aiko taught the villagers to align with nature's rhythms and embrace the flow of cosmic energy.

One day, a young man named Kaito, troubled by life's chaos, sought Aiko's guidance. She took him to a quiet river and said, "Observe the water. It flows effortlessly, embracing obstacles and finding its path. Our lives, too, must align with nature's rhythms."

Aiko showed Kaito how to meditate and listen to the wind, the trees, and the river. "Balance is key," she explained. "By tuning into the cosmic energy around us, we find harmony within ourselves."

Inspired, Kaito began to practice daily, feeling a deep connection to the universe. He learned to live in harmony with nature, finding peace and balance in the flow of cosmic energy.

As seasons passed, Kaito's life transformed. He became a source of calm and wisdom in the village, passing on Aiko's teachings. Together, they lived in harmony with the universal forces, embracing the natural flow of life.

Some see life as a journey of spiritual growth, where healing and expanding our consciousness leads to enlightenment. Through self-reflection and understa-nding our connection to everything, we pursue deeper knowledge.

In a peaceful forest, there lived a healer named Aria who believed life was a journey of spiritual growth.

One day, Leo, a young man weighed down by life's burdens, sought Aria's guidance. She led him to a tranquil meadow and said, "Life is a journey of spiritual growth. By healing and expanding your consciousness, you can reach enlightenment."

Aria taught Leo how to reflect on his inner self, to listen to the whispers of nature, and to recognize his connection to all things. "Understanding this connection," Aria explained, "is the key to deeper knowledge and true peace."

As Leo embraced these practices, he began to heal. His consciousness expanded, revealing profound insights and a sense of interconnectedness with all life. He felt a deep, transformative enlightenment.

Empowered by this experience, Leo returned to his community with a new sense of purpose. He shared his journey, inspiring others to seek their own paths of spiritual growth. Together, they embraced the journey of healing and expanding consciousness, collectively moving towards enlightenment.

The ancient Indian scriptures provide a profound roadmap to life's purpose, intricately detailing four distinct stages each individual can traverse to achieve desire, pleasure, righteousness, and, ultimately, liberation. This timeless wisdom offers a structured approach to personal and spiritual growth, which remains relevant even in today's rapidly changing world.

DESIRE

PLEASURE

RIGHTEOUSNESS

LIBERATION

STUDENT STAGE

HOUSEHOLD STAGE

RETIREMENT STAGE

RENUNCIATION STAGE

The journey begins with the ***Student Stage*** where the foundation of one's life is built. This stage kicks off when an individual is ready to absorb knowledge and skills, usually within the serene confines of an Ashram.

An ashram is a spiritual hermitage or a monastery, It's a secluded place where spiritual seekers or practitioners retreat to for spiritual growth, study, meditation, and contemplation.

---

under the guidance of a guru. The emphasis here is on cultivating discipline, necessary for focused learning, and respect for both the knowledge acquired and the mentor imparting it. Despite its apparent simplicity, the modern era frequently overlooks these fundamental virtues.

Next comes the ***Household Stage*** marking a transition from student life to establishing a family and using acquired skills to contribute to the broader community. This phase isn't just about building personal wealth but also involves sharing prosperity for improvement of society.

The third phase is the ***Retirement Stage***, this represents a withdrawal from active household responsibilities after fulfilling roles such as a parent or spouse, to focus on mentoring the younger generation and relinquishing personal desires. While the concept is straightforward, implementing it in the complexities of the modern world can be quite challenging.

The culmination of this philosophical path is the ***Renunciation Stage*** where individuals may choose to join a monastic order, dedicating their lives to deeper spiritual pursuits. This stage is accessible not only from the preceding ones but also directly from childhood for those rare souls who possess a clear and profound calling. This final stage is designed to lead to ultimate liberation.

These stages, described in the ancient texts, guide individuals through a life well-lived, ensuring that the essence of these teachings remains applicable even as times change.

"Using these four steps in Mary Smith's path to freedom in today's world."

The Ashram of Modernity

In the heart of Silicon Valley, amidst bustling startups and tech giants, Mary Smith embarked on her journey not in a traditional Ashram, but at the University of Technology. As a bright and eager computer science student, Mary's version of the Student Stage was filled with coding boot camps, hackathons, and mentorship under leading innovators. Her disciplined approach to her studies and profound respect for her mentors prepared her for the complexities of the tech world, emphasizing the ancient virtues of focus and respect in a modern context.

The Household Stage

After graduation, Mary co-founded a tech company that developed sustainable energy solutions, combining her technical skills with a desire to contribute positively to the world. As her business flourished, she married and started a family. She balanced her roles as a CEO, wife, and mother, investing her earnings not only in her family's future but also in community projects. Mary's household stage was marked by creating and sharing wealth, embodying the traditional values in a contemporary setting.

Retreat into the Forest

Years passed, and Mary's children grew up and her company matured. With a competent team in place, she transitioned into stepping back from daily operations to focus on mentoring young entrepreneurs. This phase was her symbolic retreat to the forest, withdrawing from the frontline but not from her purpose. She spent her days guiding the next generation and exploring more about renewable resources, ensuring her life's work would thrive in her absence. This stage was her slow and graceful movement away from worldly attachments, toward a broader vision of legacy and impact.

The Path of Renunciation

Finally, as her mentoring bore fruit and her company stood as a testament to sustainable practices, Mary felt a deeper call to the Renunciation Stage. She handed over her corporate responsibilities and founded a non-profit dedicated to global energy education. Her renunciation was not about isolation but about dedicating herself entirely to lifting others through her expertise, inspiring solutions to energy crises worldwide. Mary traveled, spoke, and lived modestly, her life stripped of former business attire but rich with purpose and fulfillment.

A Modern Sage

Mary's journey through the four stages did not just fulfill her desires but transformed her into a leader who transcended the typical definitions of success. Her story became one of a modern sage who navigated the complexities of the 21st century while adhering to ancient wisdom. Through her life, she demonstrated that the path laid out in age-old scriptures could indeed be walked in the corridors of modernity, leading not just to personal liberation, but to the liberation of others through knowledge and empowerment.

Mary's story is a testament to the enduring relevance of ancient philosophies in modern leadership, offering a blueprint for meaningful success in today's world.

The GURU

The term combines the two root syllables: "gu," meaning darkness or ignorance, and "ru," represents the act of destruction.

A Guru is someone who dispels darkness or ignorance.

The Word "guru" originates from Sanskrit, an ancient language of India where it holds profound spiritual significance. Historically, the concept of the guru is deeply embedded in Indian spiritual and educational traditions. The guru is revered as a teacher, spiritual leader, and guide who imparts knowledge to students and disciples. This relationship between a guru and a disciple is considered sacred and is central to the learning process in many Eastern philosophies.

Over time, the word "guru" has transcended its eastern spiritual origins and has been adopted globally in various contexts. It is often used colloquially to mean an expert or authority in a particular field, such as a business guru or a tech guru. This broader usage retains the core connotation of someone who dispels ignorance and leads others toward greater knowledge and understanding.

Ancient Indians believed that anyone or anything, including nature, capable of enlightening us or providing significant insights into life could serve as a guru.

This tale dates back thousands of years. A group of disciples were reflecting on the exceptional qualities of their guru. Curiosity arose among them: if their guru was indeed so remarkable, what about the guru of their guru? Eager to learn more, they approached their guru, who consented to share his own experiences.

My First Guru: A thief

He revealed that his first guru was a thief, which initially shocked the disciples and led them to think their guru was teasing them.

However, the guru was earnest. He recounted an evening when exhausted and needing rest while walking in a secluded area, he encountered someone and asked for help. The individual, though a thief, readily offered him shelter. As an ascetic who had renounced worldly possessions and had nothing to lose, the guru wasn't troubled by the man's confession.

He stayed with the thief for a few days, observing him closely. He noticed that the thief slept peacefully regardless of whether his day was successful or not, never allowing the outcomes to affect his contentment.

From this experience, the guru understood the importance of staying unaffected by the pain and pleasure of life's fluctuations, and thus, he considered the thief as his first teacher.

Laura's Guru: The Car Thief

In the high-stakes environment of Wall Street, a young investment banker named Laura learned an unexpected lesson from an unlikely Guru, which profoundly shifted her approach to leadership and life.

Laura was a rising star at a prestigious investment firm, known for her sharp analysis and relentless drive to succeed. However, the relentless pressure to perform and the volatile swings of the stock market began to take a toll on her mental health and job satisfaction. Despite her success, she found herself increasingly stressed and unhappy.

One late evening, as Laura was leaving her office after a particularly rough day of heavy losses, her car broke down in a rough part of the city. Stranded and anxious, she was approached by a man who noticed her distress. Joe was dressed shabbily and looked rugged. Sensing her apprehension, he calmly offered to help. He managed to get her car running but casually mentioned that he used to be a car thief, now reformed and working as a mechanic.

Initially shocked by his admission, Laura was skeptical but desperate for help. Over the next few hours, Joe not only fixed her car but also shared his life story. He spoke about his days of uncertainty and recklessness and how he found peace and contentment by changing his path and focusing on what truly mattered to him—his family and an honest living. He emphasized how he learned to sleep peacefully at night, knowing he now lived a life of integrity, regardless of his past mistakes or current hardships.

Inspired by Joe's perspective and serenity despite his turbulent past, Laura began to reflect on her own life choices and values. She realized that her relentless pursuit of financial success was not leading to personal happiness or fulfillment. Like Joe, she needed to find peace and contentment in her achievements and the process, not just the outcomes.

Motivated by this encounter, Laura returned to her firm with a new outlook. She started advocating for a healthier work-life balance, both for herself and her team, emphasizing mental well-being and job satisfaction over mere financial gains. She implemented regular mindfulness and stress management workshops, which helped improve the team's overall morale and productivity.

Laura's transformation also led her to start a nonprofit focused on financial literacy for disadvantaged youth, teaching them how to achieve financial stability without succumbing to illegal activities. Her story, inspired by a chance meeting with a former thief, became a powerful testament to the impact of empathy, integrity, and personal peace on leadership and life satisfaction.

My second Guru: A Dog

His second guru was a dog. The disciples were again astonished. How can a dog be a guru?

The guru continued with his story. He said that one day, he saw a dog that was very thirsty and went to a river to drink water. When the dog looked at the water, it saw its reflection and became frightened, turned, and ran away. This happened a couple of times, but when he could not control his thirst anymore, so the dog went to the river and jumped into the water. The dog noticed that the reflection had vanished, but it could not swim. It started moving its legs and somehow reached the other side of the river. The guru told his disciples that by observing the dog, he learned to face the challenges in life, and that's the reason he considered the dog as his second guru.

Lena's Guru: A Butterfly

In the competitive tech industry, Lena, a software developer who started her own company, found deep inspiration from an unexpected place, which greatly helped her struggling mobile app development company.

Lena's startup focused on creating user-friendly mobile applications. Yet, it was struggling to make a mark due to intense market competition and her hesitation to deviate from mainstream business strategies. Overwhelmed by pressure and doubtful about the future, Lena often escaped to a nearby botanical garden to clear her mind and seek clarity.

One sunny afternoon, while wandering through a butterfly garden within the park, Lena's attention was caught by a butterfly struggling to escape from beneath a leaf. The butterfly tried several times to free itself, each time adjusting its approach slightly. Finally, with a determined flutter, it managed to get free and soared into the sky. This struggle and eventual triumph over its predicament struck a chord with Lena.

This moment of perseverance made Lena realize that her fears—fear of unique, untested ideas and fear of potential business failure—were restricting her company's potential. The butterfly's persistence in overcoming its obstacle reflected the innovative leaps Lena needed to embrace.

Motivated by this simple yet powerful interaction, Lena rushed back to her team with a revitalized vision. She convened her team and proposed aggressive new strategies to push the boundaries of their app designs, including venturing into augmented reality and machine learning integrations, sectors filled with uncertainties but promising significant returns.

Her bold, forward-thinking mindset rejuvenated the startup's ambitions and spirit. Over the subsequent months, these daring initiatives not only set her company apart from the competition but also drew the attention of major investors, captivated by their pioneering spirit.

The episode with the butterfly evolved into a pivotal element of Lena's leadership narrative, frequently cited as a powerful allegory for persistence and innovation in facing business challenges. Her startup didn't just survive; it flourished, becoming a testament to the idea that nature can sometimes provide the most valuable lessons in resilience and creativity in business.

My Third Guru: A Young Boy

The guru went on to describe his third Guru: a 10-year-old boy.

The disciples were puzzled, questioning how such a young boy could serve as a guru. The guru recounted an encounter where he saw the boy holding a lit oil lamp. Curious, he challenged the boy by asking where the light originated.

Without hesitation, the boy extinguished the lamp and asked the guru where the light disappeared, suggesting that its source was the same as its destination. Impressed by the boy's insightful response, the guru immediately showed his respect by bowing to him.

The guru then told his disciples that our surroundings and everyday life can be our greatest teachers. He emphasized that if we remain observant and open-minded, everything around us can direct us toward the correct path. He explained that the choice to keep our eyes and minds open or closed lies within us.

Sarah's Guru: 11-year-old Sofia

In the fast-paced world of Silicon Valley, a seasoned entrepreneur named Sarah often shared wisdom and guidance with her startup team, but she found her most profound lesson in leadership from an unexpected source—a child.

Sarah's company, a burgeoning tech firm specializing in educational software, had reached a critical juncture. While exploring innovative features for their next software release, Sarah and her team faced creative roadblocks. The pressure to continuously innovate was immense, and the team felt stuck, unsure of where to find their next big idea.

During a community outreach event organized by her company, Sarah encountered a moment that would reshape her approach to innovation and leadership. The event included a science fair where local children showcased simple yet creative projects. Among the participants was an 11-year-old girl named Sofia, who had built a small solar-powered light device.

Curious about the girl's project, Sarah approached Sofia and asked her to explain the source of the power for her device. Without missing a beat, Sofia confidently dismantled her device to show the simple wiring and the small solar panel, then quickly reassembled it. She then asked Sarah, "Do you know where the energy comes from and where it goes when it's not powering my light?" Before she could answer, she continued, "It comes from the sun, and when it's not powering my light, it's powering the earth."

Sofia's simple explanation and the profound depth of her understanding struck a chord with Sarah. She realized that innovation doesn't always come from complex solutions; often, it's about seeing the simplicity and potential in everyday elements and understanding how they can be redirected or repurposed to serve new functions.

Inspired by Sofia's perspective, Sarah returned to her team with a new approach. She encouraged them to look beyond the conventional applications of their current technologies and explore how simpler, more fundamental elements could be adapted to their projects. This shift in thinking led to breakthroughs in their software development, allowing them to integrate more intuitive, user-friendly interfaces that leveraged common behaviors and environments familiar to their users.

Sarah often recounted the story of her young guru, Sofia, to highlight a critical lesson: Innovation often lies in our ability to see the ordinary in extraordinary ways, and sometimes, the most profound insights come from the most unexpected places. The team embraced this philosophy, keeping their minds open to inspiration from all sources, no matter how unconventional.

Guru and a Leader

In Eastern traditions, a guru is traditionally a spiritual teacher or mentor who imparts wisdom and guidance on philosophical, ethical, and spiritual matters.	Ideally, a ***leader*** is someone who guides others toward achieving common goals, often in business, political, or organizational contexts.
Revered for their deep knowledge and insight into life's mysteries and for helping others achieve enlightenment or a deeper understanding of themselves	Ability to inspire, motivate, and influence people to accomplish tasks, overcome challenges, and drive forward initiatives

---

Key attribute of a Guru: Wisdom

Gurus are prized for their profound wisdom and understanding, often derived from extensive study, introspection, and experience.

A Tale of CEO John and Guru Amara

John, a young and dynamic CEO of a burgeoning tech startup, found himself at a crossroads. Under his leadership, the company had achieved rapid growth and was the envy of many. Yet, John felt a deep-seated unease. The relentless pursuit of growth had led to stressed employees, a narrow focus on profits, and a gradual erosion of the company's core values.

During a visit to India to explore new markets, John encountered Guru Amara, an elderly sage known for his profound wisdom and calm manner. Intrigued by Amara's reputation, John sought his counsel, hoping to find strategies to steer his company through its cultural and ethical dilemmas.

Sitting under the ancient banyan tree in Amara's ashram, John poured out his concerns. Guru Amara listened intently, his eyes reflecting a deep understanding of the unspoken. When John finished, Amara spoke softly, his words slow and deliberate.

John," he began, "true leadership is like the banyan tree under which we sit. Its strength lies not in its height but in its roots. A leader must nurture the roots—your company's values and the well-being of its people. Growth, when not rooted in values, is like leaves without a tree, fleeting and fragile."

He continued, "Learn to balance practical needs with deeper values and consider the present and the future. Treat your employees as individuals with their own goals, not just parts of the company. Support their development, and your business will thrive."

Taking the lesson to heart, John returned with a new vision. He instituted policies that prioritized employee well-being and ethical practices. Meetings began with mindfulness exercises, and the company set aside time for volunteer work, building a sense of community and shared purpose.

Months turned into years, and the company not only retained its edge in innovation but was also hailed as one of the best places to work. Productivity and profits increased, not through forceful exertion, but through the harmonious balance of welfare and work, echoing the guru's wisdom.

Key attribute of a Guru: Guidance

They focus on their followers' spiritual growth, aiming to enlighten them on their personal and spiritual journeys.

The Transformation of CEO Maria and the Guidance of Guru Lakshmi

In today's rapidly evolving global landscape, the spiritual wisdom of traditional gurus can provide an essential compass for modern leaders. Here's a story that illustrates how a contemporary leader can integrate these age-old teachings into her leadership style to foster a deeper, more meaningful connection with her team and guide their collective spiritual growth.

Maria, the CEO of a leading sustainable energy firm, was celebrated for her innovative strategies and commitment to environmental causes. Despite her success, she felt something crucial was missing in her leadership—her team was productive, but their work seemed devoid of deeper purpose and joy.

Seeking a new perspective, Maria decided to retreat to a monastery in Bhutan, where she met Guru Lakshmi, a revered spiritual teacher known for her wisdom in integrating spiritual practices into daily life. Maria shared her concerns with Lakshmi, hoping to discover how she could bring a more profound sense of purpose and fulfillment to her team.

Lakshmi listened carefully before offering a deep but simple idea: "True leadership involves caring for both the spirit and the mind. It means leading from a place of inner peace and clarity. To guide others effectively, you first need to connect with your inner light."

Inspired, Maria returned with a renewed vision. She started integrating quiet moments of reflection into the workday and encouraged her team to set not only career goals but also personal growth objectives. She introduced mindfulness training workshops that focused on developing compassion and self-awareness, tools her team could use both in and out of the office.

As these practices became embedded in the company culture, Maria noticed a significant transformation. The office became a place of greater calm and creativity. Team members were not only more productive but also more supportive of each other, sharing a bond that went beyond mere work relations.

To deepen this shift, Maria began organizing yearly retreats where the team would spend time in nature, disconnected from technology and the pressures of daily business. These retreats included sessions on meditation and yoga and discussions on topics like ethical living and the importance of community and environmental stewardship.

These changes led to a stronger, more cohesive team that approached their work with enthusiasm and a sense of shared mission. The company's projects began to reflect this deeper engagement, leading to innovative solutions that earned the firm global recognition for both its business and ethical practices.

From Guru Lakshmi, Maria learned that spiritual growth and business success are not mutually exclusive but are, in fact, complementary.

A key attribute of a Guru: "Teaching by example

Gurus often teach through personal example, demonstrating principles of living through their actions and behaviors.

The Story of Vanessa and Her Culinary Empire

Vanessa, a celebrated chef and owner of a successful farm-to-table restaurant chain, has always advocated for sustainability and ethical sourcing in the culinary industry. She believes in the importance of locally sourced, organic ingredients and is a vocal critic of food waste and environmental degradation. However, she began to realize that her lifestyle and some of her business practices did not fully align with these publicly championed values.

During a trip to India to explore regional cuisines and sustainable farming practices, Vanessa met Guru Anil, a respected figure known for his deep commitment to living harmoniously with nature. Guru Anil not only preached about sustainable living but demonstrated it through his daily actions. He lived in a self-sufficient community where everything from food to energy was produced locally and sustainably. His profound respect for nature and dedication to minimal environmental impact inspired Vanessa deeply.

Motivated by Guru Anil's example, Vanessa returned with a renewed commitment to transform both her personal life and her business to reflect her beliefs about sustainability truly. She began by overhauling her restaurants' sourcing policies, insisting on 100% local and organic produce and implementing strict guidelines to minimize food waste. She also started a composting initiative at all her locations to recycle organic waste.

On a personal level, Vanessa moved to a smaller, more energy-efficient home and began growing some of her food. She started using public transportation and cycling to work, reducing her carbon footprint significantly. She shared these changes through a monthly newsletter to her customers, detailing her journey towards a more sustainable lifestyle and business practice.

Vanessa's commitment had a ripple effect throughout her restaurant chain. Inspired by her example, her employees started adopting more sustainable practices. Her customers appreciated her honesty and commitment, which enhanced the restaurant's reputation and customer loyalty.

Furthermore, Vanessa launched a community program that offered cooking classes focused on sustainable cooking techniques, including how to reduce food waste and use local ingredients creatively. This initiative not only strengthened her community's skills and knowledge but also highlighted her leadership in promoting sustainability in the culinary world.

Authenticity in Leadership: Vanessa learned that true leadership means practicing what you preach, which builds trust and credibility.

Community Engagement: Vanessa's efforts to educate and involve her community reinforced the impact a leader can have beyond their immediate business.

Transparent Communication: Sharing her journey with customers not only humanized her but also inspired others to reflect on their own practices.

Continuous Improvement: Vanessa showed that leadership involves ongoing efforts to align more closely with one's values, acknowledging that it is a continuous journey.

Vanessa's transformation showed how a leader could draw inspiration from traditional gurus to live a life that teaches by example, thereby fostering a culture of integrity and sustainability that resonates with both employees and customers.

A key attribute of a Guru: "Holistic Approach"

Their teachings typically encompass a holistic view of life, integrating mind, body, and spirit.

The Story of Daniel and His Tech Consulting Firm

Daniel, the CEO of a fast-growing tech startup, had always been driven by metrics and milestones. Under his leadership, the company had seen unprecedented growth, but this success came with high stress and a demanding work culture that left little room for personal well-being. Despite his accomplishments, Daniel felt something crucial was missing—not just in his life but in the very fabric of his company's culture.

Seeking a new perspective, Daniel decided to attend a leadership retreat in Bali, known for its peaceful setting and innovative workshops on transformative leadership. It was here that he met Guru Isha, a spiritual teacher whose presence radiated calm and whose teachings were revered across continents.

Guru Isha led her sessions under the cool shade of palm trees, her voice as soothing as the ocean breeze. She spoke of leadership not just as a skill but as an art that required harmony between mind, body, and spirit.

Her philosophy was that true leadership began with inner balance, and this balance was the mirror reflected in every aspect of life, including business.

"Consider a company as a living organism," Guru Isha explained. "When its leaders ignore their well-being, the entire organism suffers. Stress, burnout, and disconnection are the symptoms of a deeper imbalance. But when leaders nurture their whole selves, they cultivate an environment where creativity, passion, and resilience thrive."

Daniel was struck by the simplicity and depth of her words. He had always separated his well-being from his professional responsibilities, believing that sacrifice was a necessary component of success. But Guru Isha's teachings illuminated a different path, one where these elements were interconnected and interdependent.

Inspired, Daniel returned to his company with a renewed vision. He initiated changes that at first seemed radical to his team. He introduced flexible working hours and mandatory breaks to disconnect and rejuvenate. He invested in wellness programs that included meditation sessions and weekly yoga classes right in the office premises.

Perhaps the most significant change was the shift in how meetings were conducted. Instead of back-to-back sessions in a conference room, teams met for walking meetings in nearby parks, fostering a relaxed environment that encouraged open communication and creative thinking.

Initially, there was skepticism. Productivity seemed to dip, and some board members questioned Daniel's new approach. But as weeks turned into months, a transformation was evident. Employee morale soared, innovative ideas surfaced, and the quality of work improved dramatically. The company not only retained its top talent but became a magnet for visionary thinkers who shared the same values of balance and holistic well-being.

The holistic approach also reshaped the company's products. They developed solutions that emphasized user wellness and sustainability, aligning with their internal culture. This not only differentiated them in the marketplace but also resonated with a growing demographic of consumers who valued ethical and mindful business practices.

Under Daniel's leadership, the company emerged as a pioneer in the tech industry, one that didn't just sell products but promoted a lifestyle of balance and well-being. Daniel often reflected on his time with Guru Isha. He realized that the key to revitalizing his company was not in pursuing more aggressive targets or longer hours but in fostering an environment where everyone could thrive together in complete harmony. This was not just a new business model but a new way of living inspired by the wisdom of a spiritual teacher in Bali.

Why do Leaders Exist?

It was my second week at an organization; I found myself standing in front of the senior leadership team, leading training on Gemba Walks. (*The concept of Gemba Walks, originating from the Japanese manufacturing principles, refers to leaders going to the real place where work happens to observe, engage with employees, and understand operations firsthand*)

I was relatively new, just two weeks into my role, while most of the team members had been with the company for over a decade.

To start the session, I posed a seemingly simple set of questions:

"Why do you exist in the organization?

As senior leaders, why do you go to the office every day?

What is your purpose in the organization?"

The room was silent for over two minutes, a period that felt surprisingly long. I gave them time to reflect.

Gradually, they started to share their thoughts. Some discussed setting goals and planning, while others mentioned meeting customer needs or providing for their families.

Their responses were thoughtful yet varied, and I noticed that I stood in front of the KPI (Key Performance Indicator) management board, which was divided into categories: Safety, Quality, Delivery, Productivity, and Engagement.

Taking the opportunity, I challenged them to identify the most crucial category for the Leadership team. Silence filled the room again as they found it difficult to agree on one key metric.

Some prioritized safety, the quality leader focused on quality, and the supply chain leader emphasized delivery, whereas the operations leader argued that cost was the most important. However, engagement was totally overlooked by all.

In just a few moments, it was evident that each leader was focused on their specific department's metrics and found it difficult to agree on a unified priority.

This exercise demonstrated the organization's level of leadership maturity: they had not yet grasped the crucial role of employee engagement as a unifying force to achieve their common objectives.

As a Leader, where is the time being spent?

"Where leaders spend their time shows the organization what is important!

The currency of leadership is "presence. "

I had the unique opportunity to work with a couple of senior leaders to uncover where they spent their time. The leaders I collaborated with for this experiment included a Vice-President, a Managing Director, a General Manager, and an Operations Director.

I began with each leader by asking a fundamental question: "What is your purpose?" As a Vice President, Managing Director, General Manager, etc., why do you exist?

I apologize if this seems repetitive. It's a very critical question.

Believe it or not, it took nearly 2-3 weeks to define and articulate their purpose simply and clearly.

Once the purpose was defined, they graciously allowed me to peek into their calendars to analyze where they were actually spending their time.

The results were startling to some and unsurprising to others.

Most leaders spent the bulk of their time firefighting, reacting to situations as they arose rather than taking a proactive or strategic approach. Less than 15% of their time was spent on proactive or strategic activities.

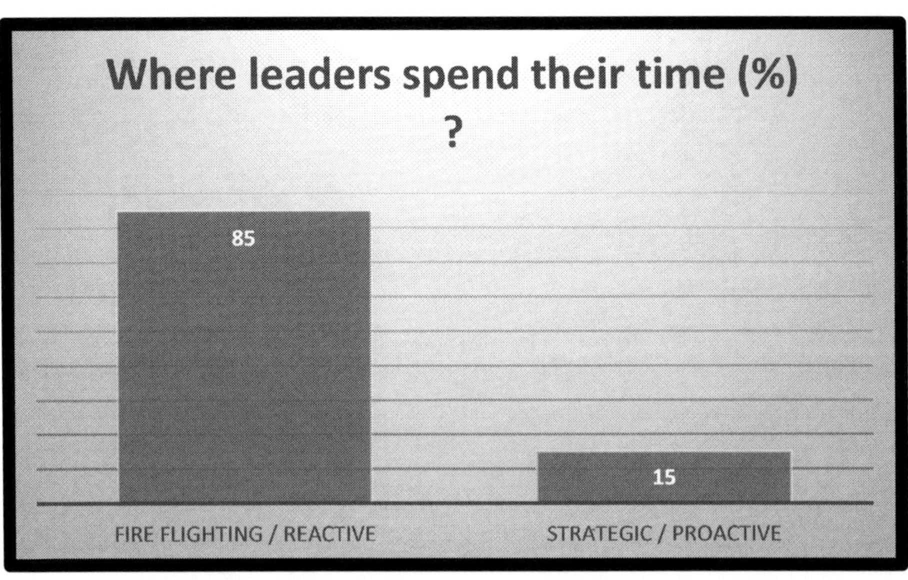
Where leaders spend their time (%)
?
85
15
FIRE FLIGHTING / REACTIVE
STRATEGIC / PROACTIVE

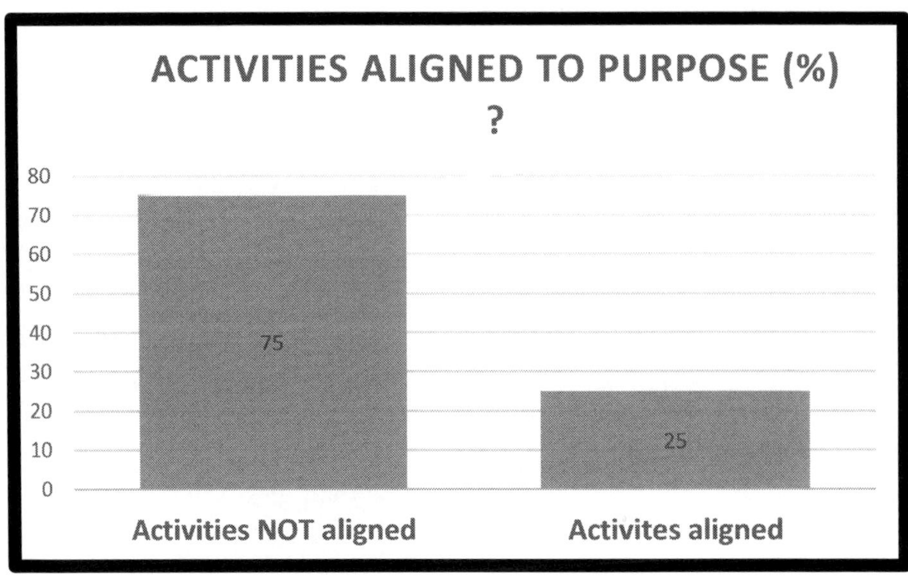
ACTIVITIES ALIGNED TO PURPOSE (%)
?
80
70
60
50
40
30
20
10
0
75
25
Activities NOT aligned
Activites aligned

The most surprising revelation, however, was more than 70% of the time leaders spent at work, didn't align with their defined purpose.

This exercise highlighted that most leaders lack clarity about their purpose, leading to a frequent disconnect between what they aim to achieve and how they actually allocate their time.

The insight has provided a valuable lesson for these leaders and for anyone in a leadership position. True leadership is about being present and aligning time with purpose, which requires a proactive approach rather than simply reacting to daily challenges.

Purpose of leadership

The primary purpose of leaders in an organization is to „Motivate" people !!

"Revitalizing Vision: How President Brian Transformed Health Life Science Through the Power of Motivation"

Once upon a time, in a bustling industrial district, there was an equipment manufacturing company known for its specialized healthcare devices. Health Life Science had been a leader in its field but began to struggle with internal issues. Morale among employees was dwindling, and productivity had slowed significantly. The workforce felt disconnected from the company's mission, especially after a recent high-stakes project failed.

In response to these challenges, Health Life Science welcomed a new president, Brian. Brian was renowned for his charismatic leadership and his track record of revitalizing underperforming companies. Upon joining the company, Brian immediately noticed that the fundamental issue wasn't the quality of their products or lack of market opportunity—it was a lack of motivation and connection to the company's broader objectives.

Brian set out to transform the company culture. He started with a series of one-on-one meetings with each team member, during which he took the time to understand their concerns and aspirations, both within and outside of their roles at the company. This approach helped him connect on a personal level, showing that he valued them as individuals, not just as employees.

Driven by the insights gained from these conversations, Brian introduced several initiatives aimed at re-engaging the workforce. He implemented a transparent communication policy that included regular town hall meetings where employees could openly discuss any concerns or ideas. He also introduced 'Innovation Labs,' a program allowing employees to dedicate time to projects they were passionate about that also aligned with the company's mission.

Additionally, Brian established a recognition program that highlighted not just successful outcomes but also the efforts and innovative methods used by employees, encouraging a culture of experimentation and continuous improvement.

Six months after these changes were implemented, the atmosphere at Health Life Science had transformed dramatically. The employees were noticeably more engaged and collaborative. The introduction of a groundbreaking new medical imaging device was a major success, earning acclaim within the healthcare sector and attracting significant interest from investors and potential partners.

Under Brian's leadership, Health Life Science became an example of how effective motivation and connecting with employees on a personal level can revitalize an organization. Brian often remarked that his primary role as a leader was to inspire and motivate, proving that the turnaround at Health Life Science was a testament to the power of a motivated workforce united by a common goal.

Purpose of Leadership

The ONLY thing of real importance that leaders do is to create and manage culture!!

"Culture at the Core: How CEO Andrea Revitalized Food Tech Corporation"

In the bustling industrial corridor, Food Tech Corporation, a food processing and packaging company, was grappling with challenges. Despite its state-of-the-art facilities and skilled workforce, the company was suffering from low employee morale and high turnover rates. The prevailing company culture was marked by strict hierarchies and limited communication, which stifled innovation and teamwork.

Recognizing the need for a significant change, Food Tech Corporation welcomed a new CEO, Andrea, known for her dynamic leadership and expertise in transforming organizational cultures. Andrea observed the existing culture of silos and the overall lack of engagement on her first day at the company. She was convinced that transforming the company culture was essential for Food Tech's success.

Andrea initiated her transformation strategy by dismantling the rigid hierarchical structures that had long dominated the company's operations. She replaced the formal, quarterly all-staff meetings with weekly informal gatherings where employees from all levels were encouraged to voice their ideas and concerns. This approach helped to break down the barriers between the management and the factory floor, fostering a sense of community and openness.

To further enhance collaboration, Andrea introduced cross-functional teams, pulling together employees from different departments to work on innovative projects. She also established a monthly "Innovation Lab Day," where employees could propose and work on new ideas that could improve the company's processes or products without the constraints of their regular job duties.

Understanding the importance of a supportive and engaging work environment, Andrea overhauled the company's core values, emphasizing teamwork, innovation, and respect. These values were integrated into every aspect of Food Tech's operations, from hiring practices to performance evaluations, ensuring they were more than just words on a poster.

Over the ensuing months, the shift in culture became evident. The workplace buzzed with renewed energy and enthusiasm. Employees felt more valued and empowered, leading to increased productivity and creativity. Food Tech Corporation successfully launched several new product lines and improved their packaging solutions, reflecting the collaborative efforts of the newly energized teams.

Under Andrea's leadership, Food Tech Corporation became a testament to how the focused management of organizational culture can rejuvenate a manufacturing company. Andrea firmly believed and often shared, "The only thing of real importance that leaders do is to create and manage culture." This belief became the foundation of Food Tech's revitalization, turning the company into a model of success and innovation in the industry.

Conclusion

Clarity of purpose is foundational to effective leadership. It acts as a compass that guides every decision, behavior, and the overarching culture within an organization. When leaders possess a deep understanding of their roles and objectives, they are better equipped to align their actions with the organization's core values and strategic goals.

This alignment streamlines decision-making and ensures that all efforts are directed towards relevant and impactful initiatives, avoiding the misallocation of resources on divergent paths.

Moreover, a clear purpose enables leaders to articulate their vision and expectations with greater precision, fostering a unified sense of direction among employees. This clarity in communication enhances motivation and engagement, as team members understand the 'why' behind their tasks and see how their contributions fit into the bigger picture. By prioritizing initiatives that resonate with the organizational purpose, leaders can maintain focus and drive, thereby enhancing overall efficiency and effectiveness.

Furthermore, clarity of purpose strengthens trust and commitment among team members. Leaders who consistently demonstrate a clear commitment to the organization's goals not only inspire confidence but also cultivate a culture of transparency and accountability. This, in turn, propels the organization towards sustained success and growth by building a resilient and motivated workforce that shares a common vision of success.

Thus, clarity of purpose is not only beneficial; it is essential for leaders who aim to foster an environment where trust, commitment, and alignment propel the organization forward.

Patience

Patience is not the ability to wait but the ability to keep a good attitude while waiting.

One minute of patience is equal to 10 years of peace.

On a recent flight to India, I found myself seated next to a seasoned consultant whose expertise was sought by Fortune 500 companies worldwide.

As the plane sliced through the clouds, we discussed the intricacies of professional patience, especially in dealing with clients at different phases of business growth. He recounted a personal story that highlighted his method of developing patience.

Every year, he explained, he would take his young grandson to the sandy shores of India. These trips were not just vacations but were sessions of patience training. His grandson, full of curiosity typical of a six-year-old, bombarded him with endless "why" questions as they built sandcastles and watched the waves. Initially, the volley of inquiries tested his temper, but he committed to responding without frustration.

As the years rolled on, these beachside dialogues transformed him. Each question patiently answered strengthened his "patience muscle," a skill that profoundly enhanced his interactions with his clients. He learned to navigate their varying levels of maturity and understanding with the same calm he used to explain the tides to his grandson, turning each client meeting into a more productive and pleasant experience.

Impatience, panic, and Hasty decisions

Once, at a business conference, I began talking to an experienced operational leader who appeared quite distressed. As we discussed leadership and performance, he expressed frustration over a recent hiring decision that hadn't worked out well. Intrigued, I asked him why he had chosen the employee he was now unhappy with.

He confessed that there had been pressure to fill the position quickly. His department faced a potential budget cut for the upcoming fiscal year, and he feared that any delay in hiring would result in a reduced headcount. So, he made a hasty decision to hire to protect his existing resources.

I asked him to reflect on whether filling the position hastily was worth it compared to the potential reduction in headcount. With a sigh, he admitted that he would have been better off with fewer team members than dealing with the underperformance and the strain it brought.

This conversation led us deeper into the realms of decision-making processes, where he revealed a crucial insight. Had he not rushed, his alternative would have been to promote and train an internal candidate—a potentially more rewarding but time-intensive option. His ultimate realization was poignant: his lack of patience not only cost him in terms of team performance but now required even more time and energy to manage the situation.

This encounter vividly illustrated how impatience in decision-making can lead to longer-term challenges and regrets, underscoring the importance of thoughtful, patient leadership.

Hiring Patience: Secret of successful organizations

The secret of successful organizations is a patient approach to hiring employees. Their thorough selection process is specifically designed for each job opening.

Here are the five key skills they typically look for :

Listening Skills: Unlike many companies, they test listening skills by asking candidates to listen to a speaker for two minutes and then recount what was said. This simple exercise is surprisingly challenging.

Problem-Solving Skills: Fundamental to success, this involves up to two days of simulations in a workplace setting to evaluate a candidate's ability to identify issues and devise solutions.

Teamwork: Candidates are assessed on their ability to collaborate within a team. This includes how they respond to others' ideas and work with different personalities.

Initiative: They seek individuals who proactively generate improvement ideas and go beyond the call of duty. Candidates are evaluated on this trait to see how they add value and pursue self-development.

Leadership: This crucial skill is assessed through exercises that simulate real-life challenges to test how candidates handle issues, ask probing questions, and prioritize fact-finding over assumptions. Leadership at these companies also involves seeing the value in each team member and leading with that mindset.

This hiring process can take 6-12 months, reflecting the company's commitment to finding the right match for its needs. Former employees often express pride in being selected through such a rigorous process.

This patient approach contributes to long-term employee retention and a strong reputation for customer satisfaction in a rapidly changing world.

The art of knowing how to wait, respecting time, and giving a pause when needed is more important when it comes to our thoughts.

Impatience coupled very often with anger, stress, and frustration ultimately ends with hasty decisions.

The Value of Patience

I learned the value of patience during a 10-day Vipassana meditation course. This intensive program requires participants to meditate for about 10 hours a day, often in complete silence, focusing on the breath. The first day was particularly challenging, but each subsequent day became slightly easier.

Vipassana is a systematic process established by Gautama Buddha over 2,500 years ago and handed down through generations. The course is designed to produce specific outcomes, emphasizing the importance of following the process without rushing for immediate results. Initially, I was preoccupied with the results, but I soon realized that by concentrating on my breathing and being present in the moment, I could naturally calm and clear my mind.

By the end of the ten days, I not only appreciated the structured process but also understood that patience was crucial to achieving lasting benefits. Each day's patience built upon the next, helping me not just to calm my mind—which is considered only 50% of the success—but also to purify it. This experience profoundly changed my view and respect for patience.

"Steady and Mindful: How Mathias Mastered Patience to Transform Operations"

Mathias, the VP of Operations at a manufacturing company, was leading a pivotal project aimed at launching a new product line and optimizing the production process, all within a tight deadline. Faced with numerous challenges, such as equipment failures and supply chain issues, the project demanded continuous adjustments and significant effort from his team.

To better manage his stress and improve his leadership skills, Mathias decided to attend a leadership retreat that included a program focused on developing mindfulness and deep focus. This program involved intensive daily exercises that trained participants to concentrate on the present moment and develop a disciplined, patient approach to personal and professional challenges.

Initially, Mathias found it difficult to shift his focus away from the project's pressing deadlines and high stakes. However, as the program progressed, he learned to anchor himself in the current moment, shifting his attention from the end goals to the processes at hand. This shift helped reduce his anxiety and significantly improved his decision-making abilities.

By the end of the retreat, Mathias's perspective had changed markedly. He not only adopted a more composed demeanor but also recognized the importance of patience in managing complex operations. Upon returning to the plant, he applied these principles to his project management approach, emphasizing careful, incremental progress over hurried efforts.

This strategy not only led to the successful introduction of the new product line but also helped instill a culture of patience and focus among his team. This transformative experience profoundly altered Mathias's approach to leadership, highlighting the strategic value of patience in the manufacturing sector.

Developing Patience: By Slowing Down

The Monk and the Overeager Disciple

In a small monastery perched atop a serene hill, an old monk was revered for his wisdom and calmness. Among his disciples was a young man who was always in a hurry, seeking quick answers to the deep mysteries of life.

One day, the disciple approached the monk, visibly frustrated. "Master," he said, "I have been meditating diligently every day, but I do not feel any closer to enlightenment. What am I doing wrong?"

The wise monk smiled gently and asked the young man to follow him. They walked to the nearby forest, where a small stream flowed quietly. The monk picked up a clear glass jar and scooped up some muddy water from the stream, then sealed it with a lid.

"Watch," said the monk, placing the jar on a flat stone. Both the monk and the disciple sat before the jar, silently watching. As the minutes passed, the mud gradually settled at the bottom, leaving the water clear and transparent.

The monk then spoke, "Just as the mud settles when the water is still, your mind will find clarity if you allow it time to settle. Patience is not about passively waiting but about being still enough to let the process unfold at its own pace."

This lesson struck a chord with the disciple, who began to appreciate the value of slowing down and allowing his spiritual journey to progress one step at a time.

Precision and Patience: Dietmar's Lesson in Mastering Manufacturing Processes"

In a large manufacturing plant known for its precision engineering, there was a seasoned operations manager named Dietmar, celebrated for his methodical nature and calm leadership. Among his team was a young engineer named Angelika, who was always eager to find rapid solutions and push for immediate results.

One day, Angelika approached Dietmar, clearly frustrated. "I've been working tirelessly on optimizing our production line for efficiency, but I don't see any substantial improvements. What am I doing wrong?" she asked.

Dietmar offered a gentle smile and suggested they walk through the plant together. As they walked, they stopped by a section where a new machine was being installed. Dietmar picked up a blueprint on a nearby table and rolled it out for Angelika to see.

"Look here," Dietmar said, pointing to the detailed machine schematic. Both of them studied the blueprint, which showed layers of complex engineering schematics that required careful assembly and calibration.

Dietmar then shared, "Just as each component of this machine must be precisely aligned and given time to be properly integrated, so too must our strategies at the plant be methodically implemented and given time to show their effects. Patience is not just waiting; it's about knowing how to pace our efforts and trust the process."

This insight struck a chord with Angelika, who began to understand the value of slowing down and allowing more time for her engineering solutions to manifest effectively. This shift in approach not only improved her project outcomes but also helped her develop a more thoughtful and effective method for handling complex manufacturing challenges.

Patience in Transformation

The Gardener and the Bamboo

In a small village nestled between rolling hills and lush forests, there lived an old gardener named Tenzin. Known for his wisdom, Tenzin was often visited by people seeking advice on life's various challenges. One day, a young villager named Lila approached him, distressed by the lack of progress in her spiritual practices.

"Master Tenzin, why does growth take so long? I've been practicing diligently, but I see no progress," she lamented.

Tenzin smiled and invited her to walk with him to a part of his garden where bamboo shoots were just beginning to break through the soil. He began to tell her about the bamboo's nature.

"Bamboo is a peculiar plant. For the first few years, its growth is underground; no visible signs on the surface. But once it begins to grow above the soil, it can shoot up to 90 feet in just a few weeks."

He placed a gentle hand on her shoulder and continued, "Just like the bamboo, your spiritual growth is happening even when you can't see it. Patience is trusting in the unseen progress that leads to eventual flourishing."

Reassured, Lila learned to appreciate the unseen aspects of her efforts and understood that patience was integral to her spiritual journey.

"Roots of Success: Marco's Lesson in Patience and Growth"

"Simone, why does growth seem so slow? I've been working tirelessly, yet I don't see the results I expect," Marco confided during one of their mentoring sessions.

Simone offered a reassuring smile and suggested they take a break and look out the office window overlooking the cityscape. As they observed the bustling city below, Simone pointed to a young oak tree growing in a small, confined space between two buildings.

"Marco, look at that oak tree out there. It spends years growing its roots deep into the earth in cramped conditions before we see any substantial growth above the surface. Once it's established, however, its growth becomes more noticeable and rapid," she explained.

Simone added, "Similarly, your professional development is building a foundation even when it's not immediately visible. Your skills and experiences are like those roots, strengthening in the background. Patience is about trusting in this foundational work that will eventually lead to visible success."

Reassured, Marco began to see the hidden aspects of his efforts and learned that patience was key to recognizing and valuing the groundwork of his career growth.

Listening to Understand vs Listening to Answer

The Sage and the Impatient Disciple

In ancient India, a sage renowned for his wisdom and serenity lived. People from far and wide came to seek his counsel. Among his followers was a young disciple, Arav, who was eager but often struggled with patience.

One day, as the sage was sharing insights from the ancient texts, Arav interrupted him, hastily asking for a simpler explanation. The sage paused, giving Arav a gentle smile, and then requested that he observe silence for the rest of the day and just listen.

As the day progressed, Arav found himself increasingly frustrated, unable to voice his questions or share his thoughts. When the day ended, the sage asked him what he had learned. Embarrassed, Arav admitted he was so consumed with his frustrations that he had missed the wisdom in the teachings.

The sage nodded, explaining, "The art of listening requires patience. It allows us to absorb wisdom deeper than the surface of words. Your impatience today made you miss the essence of the teachings. Remember, listening deeply is the first step to understanding."

Arav learned that impatience deprived him of knowledge and the peace of listening. He carried this lesson forward, slowly transforming into a thoughtful listener.

The CEO and the Fast Decision

Ellen was the CEO of a rapidly growing tech company. Known for her decisive leadership, she often made quick decisions to keep up with the market. However, her pace began to alienate her team, who felt their insights and concerns were overlooked.

During a critical project, Ellen pushed forward with a new software release despite her team's warnings about unresolved issues. Her impatience for a market-first launch resulted in software full of bugs being released, leading to customer complaints and a damaged reputation.

The fallout was immediate. The company's stock price tumbled, and the trust between Ellen and her team was strained. In the aftermath, Ellen reflected on what had happened and realized that her impatience had cost the company dearly.

Determined to mend her ways, Ellen began to prioritize listening over speaking in meetings. She implemented a new rule for herself: listen fully before responding. This change helped rebuild her team's trust and restored their confidence in her leadership. Over time, Ellen's patience in listening contributed to more thoughtful decision-making, and the company recovered its position in the market.

Both stories illustrate the critical role patience plays in effective leadership, whether in spiritual guidance or the fast-paced world of technology. Patience allows leaders to fully understand the complexities of situations and people, leading to wiser and more inclusive decisions.

Listening to Understand vs Listening to Answer

The Monk and the Troubled Villager

In a serene monastery nestled in the mountains of Tibet, there lived a wise old monk known for his profound understanding and compassion. One day, a troubled villager came to him, seeking guidance for his many hardships.

As the villager poured out his woes, the monk listened intently, his eyes closed, nodding occasionally. The villager noticed that unlike others he had spoken to, the monk did not interrupt with advice or questions; he simply listened.

After the villagers had finished, there was a long silence. Expecting some profound advice, the villager was surprised when the monk simply said, "Thank you for trusting me with your story."

Confused, the villager asked, "Aren't you going to give me advice?"

The monk replied, "Today, I listened to understand your pain, not to give you an immediate solution. Sometimes, understanding is the first step to healing."

In the weeks that followed, the villager reflected on the monk's approach and realized that being truly heard was what he needed most. This realization helped him to start addressing his problems with a clearer mind.

Erika and the Company Retreat

Erika, the senior operations Leader, noticed a decline in team morale and productivity. Concerned, she organized a company-wide retreat, not for strategic planning, but for open dialogue.

During the retreat, Erika introduced a session called "Listening Circles," where each team member could speak about their experiences and challenges without interruption. Erika participated not as a senior leader but as another listener.

To her surprise, she discovered a host of minor issues and misunderstandings that had collectively led to significant dissatisfaction among her team. She had previously been too focused on quickly resolving their concerns, usually before even understanding them fully.

Motivated by what she learned, she implemented regular "Listening Circles" at the office and trained her managers to listen to understand rather than to respond or fix problems immediately.

This shift led to an innovative period for the company, where solutions came from fully understanding the problems. Employee satisfaction soared, and the company flourished, setting new standards in both productivity and workplace culture.

Both stories highlight the transformative power of listening to understand rather than listening to answer. This approach fosters deeper relationships, whether in spiritual guidance or corporate leadership and leads to more meaningful and effective solutions.

The Master Potter and the Clay

In a quaint village nestled beside a winding river, there lived an old master potter renowned for his exquisite pottery. His skill had been honed over decades, and his patience was as legendary as his artistry. One autumn, a young apprentice, eager to master the craft, came to study under him.

The master potter welcomed the apprentice and gave him a lump of clay. "Your first task," he said, "is to prepare this clay for the wheel. This will take several days, and you must not rush the process." The apprentice, impatient to start shaping pots, quickly prepared the clay by the next morning. Proud of his speed, he presented the clay to the master.

The master, however, found the clay too coarse and uneven. He explained, "The art of pottery, like any great transformation, requires patience and attention to detail. Rushing leads to imperfections that cannot be undone later." The apprentice was then asked to start over, this time following the slow, deliberate steps the master had outlined.

Months passed, and the apprentice learned to embrace the rhythm of patience. His pots began to reflect the beauty of his newfound respect for the process, mirroring the slow and careful preparation of the clay he had initially dismissed.

The CEO and the Green Initiative

In the bustling cityscape, the CEO of a major corporation decided to lead her company through a significant transformation toward sustainability. Aware of her industry's environmental impacts, she initiated a "Green Revolution" within her company, aiming to drastically reduce its carbon footprint.

The CEO, inspired by the parable of the master potter, understood that such a transformation would require a cultural shift and patience. She started with small, manageable changes, such as reducing waste and improving recycling processes. She also invested in long-term projects like transitioning to renewable energy sources, knowing these would not yield immediate results.

As the transformation unfolded, there were challenges and resistance. The costs were high, and the benefits were not immediately apparent, leading to skepticism among stakeholders. However, the CEO held firm, regularly communicating the long-term vision and the eventual benefits not just for the company but for society at large.

After several years, the company not only reduced its environmental impact but also strengthened its market position. Customers increasingly preferred businesses committed to sustainability, and the company's forward-thinking approach attracted innovative talent and partners. The CEO's initial patience prepared the organization to thrive in a changing economic and environmental landscape.

These stories, both ancient and modern, emphasize the transformative power of patience in leadership. The master potter teaches that great results come from careful, thoughtful preparation. At the same time, the modern CEO shows that patience in corporate transformation can lead to sustainable success and a competitive advantage. Leaders today can learn from these examples that the best outcomes often come from the willingness to invest time and care into the process, trusting that the results, though perhaps slow to emerge, will be profoundly impactful.

Conclusion

In today's fast-paced and results-driven environment, the virtue of patience in leadership is more crucial than ever. Patience allows leaders to thoughtfully assess situations, make informed decisions, and cultivate a workplace that values quality over quantity. This approach not only enhances an organization's resilience and adaptability but also fosters a culture of respect and trust among its members.

When leaders exercise patience, they create an atmosphere where employees feel valued and understood. This boosts morale, encourages creativity, and promotes a deeper sense of loyalty to the company. Leaders who listen patiently and respond thoughtfully to challenges are able to develop more effective solutions that are sustainable over the long term.

Moreover, patient leaders are better equipped to handle the complexities of today's global business environment. They are adept at navigating the slow and often uncertain process of change, ensuring that the organization remains stable and productive even in turbulent times. This is particularly important in periods of transformation, where the temptation to seek quick fixes can lead to decisions that might compromise the future health of the company.

The impact of patience extends beyond internal operations—it also enhances a company's external reputation. Organizations led by patient leaders are seen as reliable and ethical, which attracts not only customers but also top talent who are eager to work in a supportive and visionary environment.

In conclusion, patience is a key component of effective leadership. It underpins the ability to develop a forward-thinking strategy, nurture a strong corporate culture, and achieve sustainable success. As demonstrated by the story of GreenTech Solutions and other organizations, patience is not merely a personal virtue but a strategic asset that can define the legacy of a leader and the trajectory of an organization.

Silence

A seed grows with no sound, but a tree falls with a huge noise.

Destruction has noise, but creation is quiet.

This is the power of silence. Grow silently!!

In a world increasingly dominated by noise, both literal and metaphorical, the wisdom of silence in leadership can often be overlooked. The following story draws inspiration from the spiritual realm to illuminate the profound impact of quiet creation and leadership in the modern era.

The Silent Grove

In a small village nestled between verdant mountains and sprawling fields, there lived a wise old monk named Lian. Known for his profound silence and serene demeanor, Lian was a spiritual leader, deeply respected not only in his village but also in neighboring towns. He seldom spoke, but when he did, his words were always impactful, carrying the weight of deep wisdom and understanding.

One day, a young, ambitious corporate leader named Sabrina visited Lian, seeking wisdom on effective leadership. She has achieved significant success in her field, known for her dynamic approach and innovative strategies. However, she felt something crucial was missing in her leadership style—peace and genuine respect from her team.

As they walked through the tranquil monastery gardens, Lian led Sabrina to a small, secluded grove. It was peaceful, with the soft rustle of leaves and distant bird calls filling the air. At the center of this grove stood an enormous, ancient tree, its branches sprawling majestically overhead.

Lian pointed to the tree and then to several small saplings peeping from the earth around it. He then shared, "Many years ago, I planted these seeds in silence. They grew quietly, nurtured by the earth, water, and sun. This giant tree was once just like these tiny saplings. Its growth was silent but steady, unnoticed by many who visited here."

Sabrina listened intently as Lian continued, "In our world, much like in this grove, the act of creation is quiet. True growth—whether of a tree or of a human spirit—takes place silently. The fall of a tree is loud, and while it may draw attention, it marks an end, not a beginning."

"The loudest leaders may seem strong and influential, but the most profound leadership, like the growth of these trees, happens quietly. It involves nurturing, patience, and a deep connection to the values one wishes to cultivate."

Sabrina realized that her leadership style had always focused on the end results, often accompanied by the 'noise' of constant updates, feedback loops, and the hustle of meeting targets. What she missed was the 'silent growth'—the subtle, often unnoticed work her team did, their personal and professional development, and the quiet moments of creativity and problem-solving.

Inspired by Lian's words and the serene environment of the grove, Sabrina returned to her corporate world with a new perspective. She began to focus more on the process rather than the outcome, to listen more than she spoke, and to appreciate the quiet moments of her team's growth and creativity.

Under her transformed leadership, her team flourished, their productivity and creativity blooming like the silent saplings in Lian's grove. They felt more valued and understood, and their workplace transformed into a space of calm, efficiency, and respect.

The Power of Silence

The story of Lian and Sabrina reminds us that in a world where noise often overshadows substance, the power of silent growth and quiet leadership can bring about profound transformation. Just as a seed grows silently into a tree, effective leadership and creation often thrive in quietude, shaping the world in ways that noise never could.

"Embracing Silence: The Philosopher's Quest for Answers with Buddha"

A renowned philosopher once visited Buddha, inundating him with numerous questions. He confessed to Buddha that he had spent a significant portion of his life seeking answers from various individuals, only to find that their responses led to even more questions.

Buddha listened patiently and then informed the philosopher that he was prepared to answer all his questions. He asked if he was willing to pay the price for these answers. The philosopher eagerly agreed, stating he was ready to pay any price, and inquired about what the price would be.

Buddha responded, "Sit in silence near me for two years. That is the price. Do this, and I promise I will personally answer all your questions and clear all your doubts."

The philosopher accepted Buddha's terms and sat in silence daily. As time passed, his thoughts slowed, and his sense of time faded. After two years, Buddha approached the philosopher and asked if he still had any questions.

The philosopher laughed and said, "I have been sitting here for two years, and I have no questions left. Through your grace, I found answers to all my questions." In life, answers are not handed to us; they are discovered within.

Answers do not come from external sources but from within ourselves. We need to listen to our inner voice—it is the most powerful thing. When we start listening to this inner voice, we find all the answers we seek.

Embracing Silence: A Modern Leader's Path to Clarity

In a bustling corporate world, John, a highly respected CEO, found himself overwhelmed with questions and uncertainties about his company's direction. Despite his relentless efforts and consulting numerous experts, he only encountered more complexity and confusion. Frustrated, John reached out to a seasoned mentor, a former executive known for his wisdom and unorthodox methods.

The mentor listened intently as John poured out his concerns, then said, "I can help you find the clarity you seek, but there is a price to pay. Are you willing to pay it?"

Desperate for answers, John agreed without hesitation and asked what the price was.

The mentor replied, "You must spend one hour each day in complete silence for the next six months. No distractions, no phone, no work—just sit in silence. After six months, I will meet with you again and answer all your questions."

Though skeptical, John agreed to the mentor's terms. He began his daily practice of silence, sitting quietly in his office, away from the usual hustle and bustle. Initially, the silence felt awkward and unproductive. But gradually, he noticed his thoughts slowing down, and a sense of calm began to replace his anxiety.

As the months passed, John found himself gaining new insights during these silent hours. Ideas that once seemed elusive began to crystallize in his mind. His decisions became clearer, and his leadership more decisive. The constant noise and clutter of daily operations gave way to a newfound clarity.

At the end of six months, the mentor visited John and asked, "Do you still have questions?" John smiled and replied, "I have been sitting in silence for six months, and I no longer have questions. In this silence, I found the answers I was looking for."

In the modern business environment, the answers to our most pressing questions often come not from the outside but from within. By embracing silence and listening to our inner voice, we can navigate the complexities of leadership and discover the clarity we need.

"Echoes of Silence: The Monastic Journey of Thomas"

In a secluded valley, nestled among towering mountains, there stood an ancient monastery known for its unwavering devotion to silence. The monks within its walls took a vow of near-complete silence, permitted to speak only two words every decade.

A young monk named Thomas entered the monastery with a heart full of devotion and determination. He embraced the silent life, spending his days in prayer, meditation, and hard labor. The years rolled by in quiet contemplation.

After ten long years, the head monk, a wise and serene elder, approached Thomas. "You have endured a decade of silence, Thomas. What are the two words you wish to speak?" he asked gently.

Thomas looked up, his eyes reflecting a mixture of weariness and resolve. "Bed... hard," he said simply.

The head monk nodded, his expression unreadable. "I see," he replied softly and left Thomas to his silent vigil.

Another decade passed in the same routine of silence and solitude. The seasons changed, and the years seemed to blend together. Again, the head monk approached Thomas. "It has been another ten years. What are the two words you wish to speak now?" he inquired.

Thomas, looking a bit thinner and more worn, met the head monk's gaze. "Food... stinks," he muttered.

The head monk's face remained calm, his eyes showing a hint of understanding. "I see," he said again and walked away.

Ten more years drifted by, the silence more profound than ever. Thomas had now spent thirty years within the monastery's austere walls. The head monk, appearing older yet still wise and composed, approached him one last time.

"Thomas, you may speak your two words."

With a deep sigh, Thomas uttered, "I... quit."

The head monk nodded slowly, a faint smile playing on his lips. "I see why," he said with a touch of humor in his voice. "All you ever do is complain."

And so, Thomas left the monastery, his silence broken and his heart lighter, realizing that sometimes the strictest paths lead us to understand our true desires.

The Silent Guru

In a remote village in India, there lived a revered spiritual leader known as Guru Mahadev. Guru Mahadev was known for his profound wisdom and his remarkable ability to lead his disciples not through words, but through silence and action. The villagers respected him immensely, often seeking his guidance for their troubles and spiritual growth.

One day, a young disciple named Aarav joined the ashram, eager to learn from the great guru. Aarav was full of questions and was puzzled by the guru's silent demeanor. Weeks passed, and he observed Guru Mahadev tending to the garden, meditating by the river, and performing daily rituals without uttering a single unnecessary word.

Frustrated and eager for answers, Aarav approached Guru Mahadev and asked, "Master, why do you remain silent most of the time? How can we learn if you do not speak?"

Guru Mahadev smiled gently and motioned for Aarav to follow him. They walked to a nearby stream where the water flowed gently over the rocks. The guru sat by the stream and finally spoke, "Observe the water, Aarav. It flows quietly, nourishing everything in its path without making noise. It does its work diligently, and yet its presence is felt everywhere."

Aarav watched the stream, beginning to understand. Guru Mahadev continued, "True leadership is like this stream. It is not about the noise we make but the actions we take. When words are necessary, they should be like precious drops of rain, meaningful and impactful. Silence allows us to listen, to understand, and to act wisely. This is the essence of spiritual leadership."

From that day on, Aarav embraced the lesson of the silent guru. He learned to value silence and understood that leadership was about setting an example through actions, not just words.

The CEO's Quiet Revolution

In the bustling city of New York, a tech company named Innovatech was led by its CEO, Sarah Collins. Sarah was known for her calm and composed leadership style. Unlike many other executives, she was not one to dominate meetings or flood inboxes with emails. Instead, she believed in speaking only when it was truly necessary.

Innovatech was facing a significant challenge: a major project had hit a roadblock, and the team was struggling to find a solution. The atmosphere in the office was tense, with many expecting Sarah to call a high-stakes meeting to address the issue.

Instead, Sarah quietly observed the situation, attending team meetings without speaking and simply listening to her employees' concerns and ideas. She spent time walking around the office, watching her team's dynamics and efforts. After a few days, she called a brief meeting with her key managers.

In the meeting, Sarah spoke clearly and concisely. "I've observed your dedication and the challenges you're facing. I trust in your capabilities and have faith that you will find the right solution. I am here to support you in any way you need, but I believe the answers lie within this team."

Her words were few, but they carried weight. The team felt empowered and trusted, and they were motivated to tackle the problem with renewed energy. Within a week, they developed a creative solution that not only solved the issue but also improved the project's overall efficiency.

Sarah's leadership style became a model for the company. She demonstrated that effective leadership doesn't require constant talking or micromanaging. By choosing her words carefully and leading through trust and silent observation, she created an environment where her team could thrive and innovate.

Both Guru Mahadev and Sarah Collins exemplify the power of silent leadership. Whether in the spiritual realm or the corporate world, they show that true leaders inspire and guide their followers through thoughtful actions and purposeful words, proving that silence can be a powerful tool in effective leadership.

Whispers from the Grove

Echoes of the Past

In a forgotten village shadowed by ancient, whispering woods lived an old spiritual teacher known simply as "The Keeper." The Keeper was revered across lands near and far for his profound wisdom and his unique way of imparting it. Unlike many who would eagerly dispense advice, The Keeper lived by three sacred principles: never answer a question until it is asked; never answer a question with another question unless coaching; and always prefer silence to words, if silence is possible.

One quiet, starlit night, a troubled young man named Eli wandered into the woods, drawn by tales of The Keeper's wisdom. He found the old man sitting peacefully by a fire, seemingly expecting him. Trembling with a mixture of fear and hope, Eli sat down across from him, but before he could speak, The Keeper looked deeply into his eyes and then returned his gaze to the fire, saying nothing.

Hours passed with only the crackling of flames and the gentle rustle of leaves. Eli, growing impatient, finally asked, "How do I find peace in my heart?" Only then did The Keeper respond, "Why do you think your heart is not at peace?" This question guided Eli to reflect on his inner turmoil, leading him to uncover his deep-seated fears and desires, a crucial step before receiving further guidance.

Lessons for Modern Leadership

Centuries later, Veronica, a CEO of a thriving tech startup, faced a tumultuous period of growth and uncertainty within her company. Inspired by the legend of The Keeper, she adopted his principles into her leadership style. During a critical meeting where her team expressed various concerns and ideas, She practiced The Keeper's methods—she listened intently, remained silent for long periods, and waited for her team to ask direct questions before she responded.

This approach fostered an environment where her team felt truly heard and valued. By not jumping to provide answers, Veronica encouraged her team members to think critically and seek solutions independently. This not only led to innovative problem-solving but also cultivated a culture of deep trust and respect.

One day, in a one-on-one coaching session with a promising team leader, the young man expressed his frustration about not meeting his project goals. Veronica, remembering The Keeper's second principle, replied with a question instead of advice: "What do you think is holding you back from achieving your goals?" This guided the young leader to self-reflect and identify areas where he needed support, enabling him to take actionable steps toward improvement.

The Confluence of Silence and Speech

Veronica's leadership style, though initially met with skepticism, proved highly effective. Her team grew not only in numbers but also in competence and morale. The principles borrowed from The Keeper's teachings—waiting for questions to be asked, using questions as a coaching tool, and valuing silence—became the cornerstone of her leadership.

As her company continued to excel, she often shared the story of The Keeper at conferences and seminars, emphasizing the power of silence and the importance of deep listening in leadership. Her story inspired many other leaders to adopt a more thoughtful and introspective approach to their roles.

Through the tale of The Keeper and the success of Veronica's leadership, the story illustrates that principles from the spiritual world, such as patience, reflection, and intentional silence, can profoundly impact modern leadership. These timeless teachings remind us that in the fast-paced rush of today's world, sometimes the most powerful actions are those taken in thoughtful stillness.

Silence in the Boardroom: A Lesson in Humility and Strength

In the bustling cityscape of New York, a medium-sized tech company named Quantum Core has been making waves with its innovative approach to data security. At the helm is Julia, a seasoned CEO known for her sharp intellect and strategic acumen. However, her journey to embody the essence of effective leadership was marked by a pivotal moment during a crucial board meeting.

It was a chilly morning in December when Quantum Core faced what many speculated might be a turning point for the company. A significant security flaw had been discovered in their flagship product, leading to widespread concern among clients and stakeholders. The boardroom was tense, filled with anxious executives and board members awaiting Julia's plan.

As the meeting commenced, Julia opened with a clear overview of the issue and its impacts. Then, the floor was opened for discussion. Suggestions and opinions began to fly, ranging from immediate, aggressive PR campaigns to downplaying the issue until a fix was in place. With each suggestion, the room grew more chaotic and divisive.

Julia listened, her expression calm, absorbing every word. As the CEO, everyone expected her to dominate the conversation, assert her authority, and impose a solution. Instead, Julia chose a different path.

After everyone had spoken, a heavy silence fell over the room. Julia remained quiet for a moment longer, letting the silence stretch. Her team looked at her, puzzled by her lack of immediate response. Finally, she spoke, her voice calm and steady, "Thank you for your insights. I believe we need a unified approach that reflects not only our commitment to integrity but also respects the concerns of our customers and our team."

She continued, "I propose we immediately acknowledge the flaw publicly, outline our steps to rectify it and enhance our customer support to handle concerns. This issue affects all of us, and only together can we reassure our customers and restore their trust."

Her words, few but impactful, shifted the atmosphere. Her silence had not been a lack of a plan but a strategic pause, allowing her to gather diverse perspectives and form a cohesive response that aligned with the company's values.

The decision to remain silent at critical moments allowed Julia to demonstrate that leadership isn't about asserting dominance but about embodying the collective voice and wisdom of the team. By not allowing her words to reflect poorly on her team or the company during a turbulent time, she showcased a profound respect for the collaborative process.

The approach Julia advocated was implemented with remarkable success. The company's transparent handling of the situation led to a surge in client trust and loyalty. Internally, Julia's respect grew immensely. Her team admired her more for her ability to listen and integrate their insights into the decision-making process, reinforcing a culture of mutual respect and collective responsibility.

Reflecting on Modern Leadership

Julia's story is a testament to the power of silence in leadership. It highlights that sometimes, the best action a leader can take is to pause, listen, and reflect before speaking. In doing so, a leader can transform potential discord into unified, strategic action that reflects well on the entire organization, setting a standard for integrity and thoughtful leadership.

Be silent - when you don't have all the facts !!

Precision and Patience: A Lesson from the Factory Floor

In the bustling industrial sector of Detroit, a mid-sized manufacturing company named Precision Alloy Works specializes in precision metal parts, primarily for the automotive and aerospace industries. Known for its meticulous quality control, Precision Alloy has a reputation for delivering top-notch components crucial for safety and performance.

The company faced a critical challenge when a large batch of aerospace parts failed to meet quality standards during a routine inspection. The flawed parts could potentially delay a major client's production schedule, risking not only a key contract but also the company's reputation in the highly competitive aerospace sector.

Linda, the plant manager, is known for her deep technical knowledge and calm demeanor. Linda had recently taken on her role and was determined to uphold the company's standards of excellence.

Upon learning of the quality issue, Linda convened her team to assess the situation. Initial suggestions from the team included rushing through a batch re-manufacture to meet the delivery deadlines. There was immense pressure to act quickly, but Linda, knowing the stakes of aerospace component failure, decided against hastiness.

Instead of bowing to pressure, Linda initiated a thorough investigation to understand the root cause of the defects. She collaborated closely with the quality assurance team and engineers to trace the entire manufacturing process, inspecting machinery and interviewing operators.

After days of detailed analysis, they discovered that the defects were caused by a recalibration error in one of the high-precision machines. The error was subtle enough to pass initial checks but significant enough to compromise the integrity of the parts.

With a clear understanding of the issue, Linda organized training sessions for the staff, focusing on recalibration procedures and enhanced monitoring protocols to prevent future occurrences. She also negotiated with the client, explaining the situation transparently and securing an extension for delivery.

To fortify against similar issues, Linda led an overhaul of the quality control processes, integrating more rigorous checks and a peer-review system on the production floor. This proactive approach not only solved the immediate problem but also set new industry standards for quality assurance in manufacturing processes.

When the new batch was delivered, not only did it exceed the client's quality expectations, but Linda's transparency and commitment to excellence strengthened the relationship with the client. The client appreciated the honest communication and the steps taken to rectify the issue, which led to additional contracts and referrals.

Linda's story is a testament to the importance of precision and patience in leadership. By prioritizing thorough investigation and quality over expediency, she not only addressed an immediate production issue but also improved her team's operations and client relations. Her approach highlights how thoughtful leadership and a commitment to quality can lead to sustainable success and trust in the manufacturing sector.

Be silent - in the heat of anger.

In a fast-paced tech startup, project leader Mehmood faced a critical moment when a heated argument broke out among his team members during a high-stress meeting. Rather than jumping in immediately, Mehmood chose to remain silent, letting the tension dissipate on its own. He then suggested a five-minute break, asking everyone to reflect on their common goals.

When the team regrouped, Mehmood calmly encouraged a focus on constructive dialogue. This approach not only resolved the dispute but also led to successful collaboration on a major project. Mehmood's decision to use silence wisely reinforced a culture of respect and effective problem-solving within his team.

Be silent - if your words will offend a weaker person

In a bustling consulting firm, manager Li Wei chose to remain silent during a team meeting when younger analyst Chen faced harsh criticisms for his project errors. Instead of piling on, Li Wei waited until after the meeting to provide Chen with gentle, constructive feedback in private.

This approach allowed Chen to learn without feeling overwhelmed and fostered a supportive atmosphere. Li

Wei's thoughtful silence and subsequent guidance not only helped Chen improve but also strengthened trust within the team.

Be silent - when you haven't verified the story.

In a manufacturing plant, production manager Ravi heard rumors blaming a key supplier for production delays. Instead of reacting immediately, Ravi remained silent and investigated the claims. He discovered the issue was due to a shipping error, not the supplier's fault.

After verifying the facts, he clarified the situation in a team meeting, emphasizing the importance of fact-checking before concluding. Ravi's approach prevented conflict and reinforced a culture of trust and responsibility among his team.

Be silent - when it is time to listen.

In an IT company, team leader Claire usually led discussions to set software development timelines quickly. Realizing her team seemed disengaged, she chose to stay silent during the next meeting to focus on listening.

This encouraged team members to share concerns about unrealistic deadlines and discuss bottlenecks. Based on the feedback, Claire adjusted the timelines and implemented their suggestions, which improved productivity and boosted morale. This highlights the importance of listening and adapting in leadership.

Be silent - if your words would convey the wrong impression

In a high-stakes negotiation with potential investors, Richard, the CEO of a tech startup, faced pointed questions about his company's recent performance downturn. Sensing the tension and potential for misinterpretation, Richard chose to remain silent rather than offer defensive or incomplete explanations.

This pause allowed him to collect his thoughts and present a clear, factual response that highlighted the company's strategic adjustments and future growth plans. His measured silence and thoughtful reply reassured the investors, securing the funding needed. This incident underscored the importance of thoughtful communication in leadership.

Be silent - if your words would damage someone else's reputation

Sascha, a project manager in a software company, overheard a rumor about a colleague's alleged mistake that could have caused a major client to pull out. In a team meeting where the rumor began to circulate more widely,

Sascha chose to stay silent rather than contribute to the gossip despite knowing some details that could have intensified the blame.

Later, Sascha discreetly confirmed the facts, which revealed a much less dramatic situation. By choosing not to speak ill based on unverified information, Sascha preserved the colleague's reputation and prevented unnecessary workplace drama. This action reinforced the values of integrity and respect within the team.

Be silent - when you are feeling critical.

Theo, a marketing director, was initially critical of a new campaign pitch presented by a junior team member during a strategy meeting. Instead of voicing his skepticism immediately, Theo chose to remain silent and listen to the full presentation. As the discussion unfolded, he learned about the innovative research and data that underpinned the campaign's approach.

By withholding his initial criticism, Theo allowed himself the opportunity to understand the proposal's potential fully. Impressed by the team's thoroughness and creativity, he supported the campaign, which ultimately led to one of the company's most successful launches. Theo's decision to listen rather than critique fostered a culture of openness and innovation within his team.

Be silent - if you can't say it without shouting.

Christian, the head of operations at a logistics firm, was frustrated with delays in a crucial supply chain project. At a tense meeting with his team, he felt the urge to raise his voice due to the escalating pressure.

Recognizing that shouting would only worsen the situation, Christian chose to remain silent and take a few deep breaths to compose himself.

Once calmer, he addressed the team with a steady voice, asking for detailed updates and solutions to prevent future delays. This composed approach not only helped identify the root causes but also maintained a respectful and productive environment. Christian's decision to stay silent instead of shouting preserved team morale and led to a constructive resolution of the issues.

Be silent - if your words will be a poor reflection of your team and your peers.

Florian, the IT department head at a tech company, faced tough questions during an executive meeting about recent project delays attributed to his team. While his initial instinct was to point out individual mistakes and external constraints, he realized that doing so could unfairly tarnish his team's reputation and diminish their morale.

Choosing to remain silent on the blame, Florian later addressed the issues privately with his team to discuss solutions and improvements constructively. Back in the executive meeting, he focused on the steps being taken to resolve the delays and the lessons learned to prevent future issues. Florian's approach not only protected his team's integrity but also showcased their resilience and commitment to continuous improvement.

Be silent - if you have already said it more than once

Johannes, Sr Leader of an insurance company, had frequently stressed the importance of data privacy and compliance to his team. Despite his repeated reminders, a compliance review revealed ongoing gaps. At the next team meeting, instead of rehashing his previous warnings, Johannes chose to remain silent, letting the review results speak for themselves.

Confronted with the concrete findings and understanding of the potential risks to the company and its clients, the team recognized the urgency of the issue. Johannes's choice to stay silent allowed them to reflect on the importance of tightening their practices. This approach prompted a proactive enhancement of their compliance procedures, proving that sometimes silence is more effective than repeated warnings.

Be silent - when you are supposed to be working.

In a tech startup, Mia, the head of software development, noticed her team was lagging on a critical app launch due to lengthy meetings. Deciding to limit her input and shorten the meetings, Mia shifted to a listening-focused approach.

This allowed her team more time to code, significantly boosting productivity. They completed the app ahead of schedule with excellent test results. Mia's strategy of embracing silence not only sped up the launch but also enhanced team morale, showcasing the value of leadership that prioritizes action over discussion.

Be silent - when your words do not do any good to anyone, including yourself.

Samantha, a senior consultant, found herself in a heated debate during a company strategy meeting. Opinions clashed, and tensions rose as colleagues became defensive. Noticing the escalating conflict and the lack of productive dialogue, Samantha chose to stop arguing and remain silent.

This pause helped calm the atmosphere, prompting others also to take a step back and reconsider their approach. The meeting resumed with a more constructive tone, leading to a consensus that was beneficial for the entire company. Samantha's decision to embrace silence demonstrated her leadership and understanding that sometimes, the most powerful contribution is knowing when to refrain from adding to the noise.

Conclusion

In today's fast-paced and often noisy world, the importance of silence in leadership is prominent; silence allows leaders to listen more effectively, think deeply, and foster an environment where creativity and introspection flourish. By embracing quietness, leaders can make more considered decisions, better understand the needs and aspirations of their team, and cultivate a workplace atmosphere that values thoughtful deliberation over impulsive actions. This approach not only enhances team dynamics and productivity but also contributes to more mindfulness and sustainable leadership; in essence, silence is a powerful tool that, when used wisely, can transform leadership from merely effective to truly visionary.

"Silence is the Language of the Soul."

"Whoever guards his tongue keeps his soul away from troubles."

"If you cannot understand my silence, you cannot understand my words."

Simplicity

"Simplicity in leadership is the art of cutting through the noise, letting spiritual wisdom illuminate the path."

"Complex Challenges, Simple Solutions"

A wealthy man suffered from serious eye problems. Despite consulting numerous specialists and trying various medications, nothing worked. Left with no alternatives, he sought advice from a monk. The monk suggested that he should only view the color green.

Taking this advice to heart, the man had his entire house painted green and instructed his staff to wear green clothes, ensuring that everything around him was green. When the monk later visited, wearing a red robe, the man had his servants cover the monk in green paint, which shocked the monk.

Upon hearing why, the monk laughed and said, "You could have simply bought a pair of green glasses for a few dollars instead of trying to make everything around you green. This would have saved you a fortune."

The lesson here is to change our perspective rather than trying to alter the world around us. It's better to simplify our thinking and our lives.

"Simplicity in Command: Elena's Leadership Awakening"

Once, there was a CEO of a tech startup, Elena, who believed the only way to innovate was through relentless technological advancement. Her company had been struggling with coordination and workflow issues, leading to missed deadlines and frustrated clients. Determined to fix these issues, Elena invested heavily in cutting-edge project management software, believing that technology alone could solve their problems.

Months passed, and while the software was indeed sophisticated, the company's productivity issues worsened. Employee morale was low, and the team felt disconnected. Elena, perplexed by the lack of improvement, decided to seek outside advice and hired a renowned business coach, Max.

Max spent a week observing the company's operations and then met with Elena. Instead of discussing further technological enhancements, he suggested a radically different approach. "Elena," he said, "your team doesn't need more technology. They need better communication and leadership that inspires. Let's strip back some of these complex systems and focus on building a culture of open communication and trust."

Initially, Elena was resistant, but realizing her efforts were futile, she agreed to a trial period of Max's simpler strategies. She started hosting regular town hall meetings where employees could voice concerns and suggest improvements. She also initiated team-building retreats to foster a sense of community and shared purpose.

Over time, Elena noticed a significant change. Projects were completed on time, the quality of work improved, and the team members were visibly more engaged and happier. It wasn't the technology that needed to change; it was her approach to leadership.

Max's parting words to her echoed the lesson from the ancient story of the monk and the rich man: "Sometimes, changing your perspective is more effective than trying to change everything around you. Leadership is not about adding complexity, but about fostering simplicity and clarity."

Elena learned that true innovation in leadership often comes not from the tools one uses, but from the environment one cultivates. This modern parable reinforces the idea that solutions need not be extravagant or expensive; often, simplicity coupled with a shift in perspective is the most powerful tool a leader can wield.

"If you cannot explain something to a six-year-old, that means you have not understood it yourself."

Albert Einstein

The Spiritual Teacher

Long ago, in a secluded mountain village lived an elderly spiritual teacher known for her profound wisdom and simplicity. People from far and wide would visit her to seek guidance on complex issues. One day, a young scholar arrived, frustrated with the abstract theories of life and the universe he had learned in the city. He challenged the teacher, asking her to explain the nature of existence in terms a child could understand.

With a gentle smile, the teacher invited the scholar to join her on a walk the next morning. As dawn broke, they strolled together, observing the waking life around them.

They stopped by a stream, and she asked the scholar to look at the water flowing over the pebbles.

"Imagine you are a leaf floating on that stream," she said. "Sometimes the water is calm, and sometimes it rushes fast, much like our lives. The stream carries you without effort on your part. Existence is much like this stream—always moving, carrying us through different experiences. Even a child understands how to float a leaf on water."

The scholar realized that the complexities he had struggled with were like turbulent waters, and true understanding was in appreciating the natural flow of life, which was easily grasped even by a child.

The Modern Leader

In the modern corporate world, a new CEO takes the helm of a struggling multinational technology firm. The company, bogged down by complex processes and an unclear mission, was failing to innovate. During his first address to the company, the CEO presented a bold vision of streamlining operations but faced skepticism due to the perceived complexity of implementing such changes.

Remembering Einstein's words, he decided to explain his strategy through a simple analogy, understandable even to a young child. He invited the employees' children to a special meeting where he presented his plan as a game of building blocks, where each block represented a core part of the company. Just like in a game where misplaced blocks could make the structure wobble and fall, in the company, every department needed to align perfectly to build a robust business.

This simplicity in explanation resonated not just with the children, who immediately grasped the concept, but also with the employees. The CEO's approach demystified the strategic changes and illustrated the importance of every employee's role in clear, relatable terms. Morale soared, and the implementation went ahead more smoothly than anyone had anticipated, proving that true understanding comes from simplicity.

The Story of AutoComponent Co.

In the bustling world of automotive manufacturing, where precision and efficiency are paramount, there once lay a mid-sized company named AutoComponent Co. The company specializes in producing a range of critical components used in car engines and transmissions. However, AutoComponent Co. was struggling with declining profits, production inefficiencies, and increasing competition from rivals, both domestic and international.

The leadership team, under the pressure of increasing competition, initially responded by adding more sophisticated technology and complex processes to their manufacturing lines. They invested heavily in state-of-the-art machinery, advanced AI for quality control, and intricate supply chain management software. Despite these advancements, the problems seemed to multiply rather than diminish. Production times increased, maintenance costs soared, and worker satisfaction plummeted.

Enter a new CEO, Maria Thompson, who had a reputation for turning around struggling manufacturing plants. Maria believed strongly in the principle of simplicity. Her first step was to conduct a thorough review of the production processes alongside frontline employees and supervisors. Through numerous discussions, it became evident that the complexity of new technologies and processes had overwhelmed the workers, many of whom were seasoned experts in traditional manufacturing techniques.

Maria decided to shift the company's approach:

Simplify Processes: She led an initiative to strip away unnecessary steps in the production process and reduce reliance on overly sophisticated technology that did not significantly enhance productivity.

Empower Workers: Maria reintroduced manual controls to certain parts of the line, where human expertise was more reliable than automated processes. This change empowered the workers, tapping into their deep understanding of the machinery.

Focus on Core Competencies: Instead of sprawling innovation, she refocused the company's efforts on its core competencies and improved those processes, making them leaner and more effective.

The results were remarkable:

Production Efficiency: Simplifying the processes reduced production time by 20%, as workers were more familiar with the systems and could troubleshoot issues more quickly.

Cost Reduction: Maintenance costs dropped by 30% as simpler machinery required less frequent and less expensive repairs.

Employee Morale: Worker satisfaction surged due to their increased involvement in the decision-making process and the revival of their expert roles.

Under Maria's leadership, AutoComponent Co. not only resolved its immediate operational issues but also carved out a competitive advantage. By simplifying processes, the company could produce components faster and at a lower cost than competitors who were still tangled in complex, tech-heavy processes. This strategic shift helped the company regain its position in the market and attracted significant new contracts.

This story from AutoComponent Co. serves as a powerful testament to the effectiveness of simplicity in leadership and problem-solving within modern manufacturing. Maria Thompson's leadership highlights how, even in industries driven by technology and innovation, simplicity can lead to better efficiency, employee engagement, and competitive positioning.

The Monk and the CEO

In the bustling city of New York, a tech CEO named Emily finds herself overwhelmed by the complexity of her life and work. Despite her company's success, she feels something is amiss.

Seeking peace, Emily attends a talk at a local community center by a Tibetan monk named Lobsang, who is renowned for his simple but profound teachings on happiness and leadership.

During the talk, Lobsang shares a story about an ancient king who sought the secret to kingdom management. The king initially tried to control everything, from the smallest market to the largest military decisions. Over time, he realized that by simplifying his approach and focusing on key principles like justice, economic stability, and public welfare, the kingdom thrived more than it did under his strict control.

Inspired, Emily approaches Lobsang afterward. She shares her struggles with managing her company and her life, feeling as if complexity had overtaken everything.

Lobsang advises her, "In leadership, as in life, simplicity is the heart of effective strategies. Focus on what truly matters: your employees' well-being, customer satisfaction, and continual learning. Simplify your processes, meetings, and products. Let simplicity be your guide, not complexity."

Emily returns to her company with a new vision. She starts by reducing unnecessary meetings, streamlining product lines, and focusing on employee development. She also institutes 'quiet hours' during the workday for deep work without interruptions.

Over the next year, the company's productivity and employee satisfaction soared. The simpler approach allows more room for creativity and efficiency, leading to breakthrough innovations and a happier workplace. Emily also finds personal happiness by simplifying her own life and dedicating time to meditation and family.

At the next annual company meeting, Emily shares her journey of embracing simplicity. She tells her team, "We've learned that by focusing on the essentials, we achieve so much more. Complexity might seem impressive, but simplicity brings clarity and results."

This story demonstrates how simplicity can lead to profound success both in the spiritual sense and in modern leadership. By reducing the clutter and noise, both the monk and the CEO find that the essential shines through, leading to true effectiveness and inner peace. This tale serves as a powerful reminder of the transformative power of simplicity in our complex world.

The Monk's Lesson and the Innovator's Mission

The Monk's Lesson

In the serene landscapes of Kyoto, Japan, there was a Zen monastery known for its ancient teachings on simplicity and mindfulness. The monastery was led by an old monk named Kaito, who was revered for his wisdom and serene demeanor. Kaito believed that simplicity was the essence of understanding the universe and achieving inner peace.

One spring morning, Kaito gathered his disciples in the garden filled with blooming cherry blossoms. He handed each disciple a cluttered box filled with various objects: stones, leaves, papers, and random trinkets. He then instructed them, "Remove everything from the box that is not essential."

The disciples began sorting through their boxes, each trying to determine what was essential. After a while, Kaito walked around and looked into their boxes. He noticed that many still held onto several items, unable to decide what truly mattered.

Kaito then took his own box and turned it upside down, emptying its contents entirely. The disciples watched in surprise as he said, "To see the essence, you must first clear away all that clutters your vision and heart. Simplicity is not about having little; it's about freeing oneself to appreciate everything."

This lesson became a turning point for the disciples, teaching them that the path to wisdom and creativity was not through accumulating knowledge and items but through simplifying and focusing on the fundamentals.

The Innovator's Mission

Mirroring the ancient wisdom of Monk Kaito, Sarah Jennings, the CEO of a fast-growing tech startup in Silicon Valley, faced the challenge of leading her team through a period of significant technological complexity and market pressure. Sarah believed that for her company to lead in innovation, they needed to embrace simplicity in their thinking and operations.

Sarah introduced "Simplicity Days" at her company—a day each month when all employees were encouraged to work on a single task or project without the usual interruptions of meetings or emails. Before the first Simplicity Day, she shared the story of Monk Kaito with her team, explaining how clearing away clutter allowed for deeper focus and creativity.

The impact of these days was profound. Employees found that by reducing the complexity of their work environment and focusing deeply on one thing, they could come up with solutions that were both innovative and straightforward. Products designed on Simplicity Days were more user-friendly and often performed better in the market.

Seeing the success, Sarah took it a step further by simplifying the company's product lines, reducing the number of features in new releases to enhance user experience and focus on core functionalities. This approach not only differentiated their products in a crowded market but also made them easier to use, leading to higher customer satisfaction and loyalty.

Both stories, though set in vastly different environments, demonstrate the power of simplicity in achieving clarity, peace, and innovation. Whether in the spiritual realm of a Zen monastery or the dynamic world of Silicon Valley, the principle holds true: by encouraging simplicity, leaders can unlock their people's true potential and creativity.

The Foreman's Insight and the Factory's Transformation

In the industrial heartland of Germany, in a town renowned for precision engineering, there stood an old factory that had been producing automotive parts for decades. The factory was a maze of machines and conveyors, and over the years, as demand and production lines increased, the layout had become increasingly complex and inefficient.

Max, an experienced foreman who had worked in the factory as an apprentice, observed that the complexity of the plant layout was causing delays, errors, and employee dissatisfaction. He remembered a lesson from his grandfather, who used to say, "In simplicity, there is efficiency and clarity."

Inspired to make a change, Max proposed a radical idea to the management: to reorganize the factory floor based on the principles of simplicity and lean manufacturing. His plan involved stripping away unnecessary equipment, repositioning machines for optimal flow, and reducing the steps required to move parts from one stage of assembly to another.

After some initial resistance, the management agreed to a trial run of Max's plan. Over several months, Max led a team that painstakingly redesigned the factory layout. They eliminated redundant machinery, created direct pathways for materials, and introduced quality control points at critical stages of the production process.

The results were astonishing. Production times decreased, product defects were dramatically reduced, and worker satisfaction improved as the factory became a less chaotic and more harmonious place to work. Max's insight transformed the factory by embracing the power of simplicity.

The Factory's Transformation

Seeing the success of the new layout, the factory's leadership decided to apply Max's principles of simplicity across the entire company. They started by simplifying the communication processes and reducing the layers of management to enhance direct, effective interactions between teams.

This was complemented by the introduction of digital tools to streamline data management and order processing, removing clutter and reducing the time spent on administrative tasks.

Furthermore, the leadership introduced training programs focused on the principles of simplicity and lean manufacturing. Employees were encouraged to identify areas of waste and complexity in their workflows and suggest improvements. This initiative not only empowered the workers but also fostered a culture of continuous improvement and innovation.

As the factory's reputation for efficiency and quality grew, it began attracting larger contracts from major automotive manufacturers. The simplicity in operations had not only improved the internal workings but had also enhanced the factory's standing in the market.

This story from a manufacturing setup illustrates that the principle of simplicity can be as transformative in a practical, industrial context as in a more philosophical or creative one. By focusing on simplicity, the foreman was able to lead his factory into a new era of productivity and success, demonstrating that simplicity is a powerful tool for improvement in any setting.

The Sage's Path and the CEO's Journey

The Sage's Path

In a small village nestled in the Himalayas, there lived a sage named Dev, known throughout the region for his profound wisdom and serene way of living. Dev's hut was perched atop a hill, surrounded by nature, and his lifestyle was the epitome of simplicity—he owned only what was necessary, spent his days in meditation, and helped villagers.

One day, a group of young seekers from the city came to visit Dev, eager to learn the secret to his peace and clarity. Observing their complex gadgets, packed schedules, and restless spirits, Dev decided to teach them through experience rather than words.

He invited them to spend a day with him, but with one condition: they had to leave all their belongings at the base of the hill and take only themselves up the path to his hut. Reluctantly, they agreed.

As the day unfolded, Dev engaged them in various tasks—collecting firewood, preparing food, and meditating by the river. Without their usual distractions, the seekers began to notice the beauty of the nature around them, the soothing sounds of the river, and the richness of silence. By the day's end, they felt a sense of calm and clarity they had not known before.

Dev explained, "In simplicity, there is efficiency and clarity. Without the clutter of possessions and distractions, you were able to experience life more fully and understand yourselves better."

The CEO's Journey

Mirroring Sage Dev's teachings, Amanda, CEO of a bustling tech company in San Francisco, found herself overwhelmed by the complexity of her role and the constant demands on her attention. Remembering a lesson she learned during a retreat in the Himalayas, Amanda decided to apply the principle of simplicity to her leadership and company operations.

Amanda began by simplifying her company's product lines, focusing on core products that were most effective and beloved by customers rather than expanding into new, untested areas. She streamlined internal processes, reducing bureaucratic red tape and implementing clearer communication channels.

She also transformed the company culture by instituting "No Meeting Wednesdays," allowing employees to focus on deep work without interruptions. This simple change led to a significant boost in productivity and creativity within the team.

Furthermore, Amanda adopted open and transparent communication practices, simplifying how information was shared and processed within the company. This shift not only saved time but also built stronger trust and alignment among her staff.

Both the sage's way of life and the CEO's strategic leadership demonstrate the profound truth of the adage, "In simplicity, there is efficiency and clarity." By reducing physical and operational clutter, both leaders were able to enhance focus, improve efficiency, and foster an environment where clarity leads to improved outcomes and greater well-being.

The Parable of the Quiet Monk and the Executive's Epiphany

The Quiet Monk

In the serene monastic communities of Tibet, there was a monk named Tenzin, who was known for his profound silence and simple communication style. Unlike his peers, who engaged in lengthy philosophical discussions, Tenzin preferred to speak rarely, choosing his words with utmost care and intention.

One winter, a group of young monks who were frustrated with the complexities of their spiritual texts approached Tenzin for guidance. They expected detailed lectures and intricate explanations. Instead, Tenzin invited them to join him on a silent hike through the snowy mountains.

As they walked in silence, Tenzin occasionally pointed to the scenes around them—the way the snow settled on the cedar branches, the patterns of the ice in a stream, the flight of a mountain eagle. Each gesture was simple but filled with meaning, requiring no elaborate discourse to understand its significance.

At the end of the day, as they warmed themselves near a fire, Tenzin spoke his only sentence of the trip, "True understanding needs no excess of words."

The young monks realized that their spiritual complexities could often be understood in simpler, more intuitive ways. Tenzin's leadership in using minimal but meaningful communication taught them the power of simplicity in conveying profound truths.

The Executive's Realization

Mirroring Tenzin's teachings, Laura, a high-powered executive at a bustling New York advertising firm, faced challenges with her team due to misunderstandings and missed deadlines, all due to overly complicated communication and excessive meetings.

Remembering a lesson from a leadership retreat that emphasized the power of simplicity, Laura decided to change her approach drastically. She started by reducing the number of daily emails and meetings, insisting that communications be clear and concise. She introduced a new rule: no email could exceed five sentences, and no meeting could last longer than 15 minutes without a justified reason.

Laura also implemented a weekly 'silent hour,' a concept inspired by her reading about monastic practices. During this time, everyone could reflect on their tasks and projects without interruptions. This not only reduced the noise of constant emails and updates but also improved focus and productivity.

To her surprise, these changes led to a significant turnaround in team performance. Projects were completed faster, creativity soared, and the team members expressed greater job satisfaction. They had learned to communicate more effectively by saying less.

Both Tenzin and Laura illustrate that leadership involves not just the ability to direct and instruct but also the wisdom to know when words should be few. By embracing simplicity in communication, both leaders were able to foster environments where clarity and understanding thrived, proving that often, less is indeed more.

The Monk's Simple Cure

In a remote monastery in the hills of Bhutan, an elderly monk named Lama Sonam lived. He was renowned for his wisdom and simplicity. The monastery often received visitors seeking advice for their complex life issues, expecting intricate spiritual rituals or long meditative practices as solutions.

One day, a young man burdened with stress from his fast-paced city life visited Lama Sonam, hoping to find a profound spiritual remedy. He detailed his extensive daily routines and the complexities that left him anxious and exhausted.

Lama Sonam listened intently, then led the young man to the monastery garden and handed him a single, small pebble. "Carry this with you," he instructed, "and every time you feel overwhelmed, hold the pebble and think of only one thing you are grateful for in that moment."

Confused yet intrigued, the young man followed the advice. Over time, he found that this simple act significantly eased his anxiety. The solution wasn't elaborate; instead, it was a simple tool that brought him back to the essentials of life—appreciation and focus. He learned that often, the simplest solutions are the most effective.

The Executive's Streamlined Strategy

In a bustling corporate office in downtown Chicago, Thomas Reed, a seasoned executive at a multinational corporation, was grappling with declining efficiency and mounting frustrations within his team. The company had been pursuing ambitious goals with complex strategies, which led to confusion and stalled projects.

Thomas was inspired by a leadership seminar that emphasized the power of simplicity in business processes. Realizing the need for change, he introduced a new initiative called "Simplify to Amplify," which aimed at decluttering workflows and decision-making processes within his teams.

He started by restructuring the team meetings. Instead of the usual lengthy and often unproductive sessions, he implemented strict 15-minute daily stand-ups, during which each team member was asked to address a single pressing issue and suggest a straightforward, practical solution. This approach forced the team to focus on the core of the problems without getting lost in details.

Thomas also simplified reporting processes. Previously, the team was bogged down by extensive documentation requirements that contributed little to actual productivity. He reduced the paperwork to essential elements and shifted the team's focus from the quantity of reports to the quality of insights, encouraging them to present only the most pertinent information.

The changes Thomas implemented had a ripple effect throughout the organization. Projects that had been lagging for months were suddenly propelled forward with renewed vigor and clearer direction. Team members felt more accountable and empowered, knowing that their contributions were directly tied to simpler, more impactful outcomes.

Morale soared as the team saw tangible results from their streamlined efforts. Thomas's initiative was soon adopted by other departments, leading to a company-wide enhancement in productivity and job satisfaction.

The Plant Manager's Simplified Success

In an industrial complex in Detroit, known for its robust automotive manufacturing, Michael Johnson, a plant manager, was facing increasing challenges with production delays and worker dissatisfaction. The assembly lines were cluttered with outdated processes and unnecessary steps that slowed down production and confused workers.

Inspired by a recent seminar on lean manufacturing and the principles of simplicity,

Michael decided to overhaul the plant's operations radically. He introduced the concept of "Less is More" to his team, focusing on reducing waste and simplifying each step of the manufacturing process.

Michael began by mapping out all the current processes and identifying areas where complexity could be eliminated. He then organized workshops for the staff, where teams could suggest simplifications based on their daily experiences. This collaborative approach not only empowered the employees but also provided Michael with insights into inefficiencies he hadn't previously noticed.

One of the major changes involved restructuring the assembly line to follow a more logical sequence, which reduced unnecessary movement and handling. Michael also introduced better tool organization and standardized work procedures to ensure every task was performed efficiently and correctly.

Furthermore, Michael implemented a visual management system throughout the plant. This system used simple symbols and color codes to convey information quickly and clearly, reducing the time workers spent interpreting instructions and increasing their time on productive work.

The impact of these changes was immediate and significant. Production times decreased, the rate of errors dropped dramatically, and employee morale improved as workers felt more involved and valued in the process. The plant soon set new records for both output and quality and other facilities within the company began looking to Michael's methods as a blueprint for improvement.

Michael Johnson's story in the manufacturing sector mirrors the effectiveness of simplicity seen in spiritual teachings. By streamlining processes and reducing complexities, he not only improved the efficiency and output of his plant but also enhanced the working environment for his team. This approach proves that in both the spiritual and industrial worlds, simplicity can lead to profound improvements in performance and satisfaction.

Conclusion

Leadership plays a crucial role in motivating teams to embrace simplicity, a principle that significantly enhances organizational efficiency and speed.

By encouraging simpler thinking, leaders can eliminate unnecessary complexities that often bog down processes and decision-making. This streamlined approach not only quickens the pace of operations but also clarifies objectives, making it easier for teams to focus on what truly matters.

In essence, when leaders champion simplicity, they facilitate faster responses, more agile adaptations to market changes, and more efficient problem-solving.

Thus, simplicity in thought and action, driven by effective leadership, directly contributes to the speed and success of an organization's initiatives.

Discipline

"The disciplined leader find their spiritual compass in everyday rituals, leading with clarity and conviction."

Discipline is the ability to make oneself do things that one knows need to be done, even when one does not want to.

Discipline is the act of managing our own feelings and desires with the intention of improving ourselves.

Discipline is saying yes to one decision and saying no to 99 other distractions. This one decision is a commitment, and honoring this commitment comes from discipline.

"Unwavering Discipline: Lessons from a 25-Year Routine of Consistent Practice"

One of my mentors shared an intriguing routine with me, which he faithfully followed every day. At 5 AM sharp, he laced up his running shoes and embarked on his morning jog. Initially, I couldn't discern anything extraordinary about this practice. However, he elaborated, revealing the true essence of his ritual.

He explained, "Come rain or shine at 5 AM, I don my running shoes and head out for my jog. Whether the world is blanketed in snow or I wake up in a foul mood, I stick to my routine. Even on the windiest of mornings, I'm out there, running. For the past 25 years, without fail, I've upheld this ritual." Never missed a day !!

What struck me most was his unwavering commitment and proficiency. Reflecting on the journey of competency, from unawareness to mastery, I realized my mentor had reached the pinnacle: unconscious competence. Much like the routine act of brushing teeth or driving a car, his discipline had become ingrained to the point where it was second nature. It was a fascinating insight into the power of consistent practice and self-discipline.

A day in the life of a Buddhist monk - the Shaolin

Monks experience a higher level of overall well-being and inner tranquility, making their way of life a source of motivation for many globally.

The Shaolin Monastery in China, a Zen Buddhist temple over 1500 years old, is renowned worldwide. Monks begin their day at 5 AM and conclude at 11 PM, dedicating

18 hours daily to three principal activities: study, practice, and service.

Study involves deepening their understanding of Buddhism

Practice is dedicated to enhancing physical and mental strength through kung fu and meditation.

Service includes maintaining the monastery by cleaning, cooking, and performing other duties.

This rigorous daily schedule demands substantial self-discipline, which monks cultivate by embracing specific life attitudes. They manage with minimal facilities, such as washing clothes by hand without running water, fostering a sense of gratitude for the simplest aspects of life.

This appreciation for minor details significantly boosts their psychological well-being, fostering a positive outlook on life and enhancing their ability to fulfill their objectives and purposes.

The second method monks use to cultivate self-discipline involves altering their perspective on materialism and wealth, leading to the understanding that happiness isn't derived from material possessions or wealth. Through this process, monks come to recognize that true satisfaction and mental peace stem from embracing a passion or life's mission. The core message is that clarity on your purpose and goals means it's not wealth driving you but rather your passion propelling you toward your objectives. Even during challenging times, when progress seems slow, having a clear purpose bolsters your self-discipline.

Traditionally, monks have always been prepared to defend their temple if necessary. This readiness continues today, with training that ensures they maintain physical and mental balance without overexerting themselves to the point of pain or injury. They believe that any physical ailment could compromise their preparedness for any threats. Thus, disciplined self-care and adequate rest are integral to their regimen.

Despite their unique lifestyle, Shaolin monks share one common trait with many productive individuals globally: they adhere to a daily routine, underscoring the significance of self-discipline.

The Mindful Leader: A Story of Transformation at PrimeEquip

Emily Larson, the newly appointed senior vice president of Operations of Ideal Moulds Inc., a prominent manufacturing company, was eager to make a positive impact. Despite the company's robust performance, she noticed a pervasive sense of burnout and disengagement among employees. Determined to foster a healthier work environment, Emily sought advice from a trusted mentor, Master Li, a renowned monk known for his teachings on mindfulness and appreciation.

During their meeting, Master Li shared a simple yet profound insight:

"Taking the time to appreciate small, positive things can have a major impact on building psychological momentum. Leaders should schedule time in their daily routines to recognize the small, positive actions or improvements their teams are making."

Inspired by these words, Emily decided to integrate this philosophy into her leadership approach at Ideal Moulds Inc.

Emily began by adjusting her daily routine. Every morning, she dedicated the first 30 minutes of her day to reflecting on the previous day's small wins and positive actions within the company. She jotted down notes about team members who had gone above and beyond, innovative solutions that had been proposed, and small but significant improvements in processes.

Armed with this positive focus, Emily made it a point to walk the factory floor daily. She acknowledged and thanked employees for their contributions, whether it was a new idea from an engineer, a quality improvement from a production worker, or a supportive gesture from a colleague. These genuine, heartfelt recognitions began to ripple through the organization, slowly changing the atmosphere.

To further embed this practice, Emily introduced "Appreciation Moments" in team meetings. At the start of each meeting, team members shared something positive they noticed about their colleagues or the work being done. Initially, it felt awkward, but over time, it became a cherished part of their routine, fostering a culture of mutual respect and recognition.

One such moment involved Sarah, a line supervisor, who had noticed a team member, Jack, staying late to ensure a critical order was completed on time. During a meeting, Sarah publicly appreciated Jack's dedication, which not only boosted Jack's morale but also inspired others to put in their best efforts.

Emily also implemented a digital "Kudos Board" where employees could post notes of appreciation for their colleagues.

This board became a visual testament to the positive contributions happening daily, reinforcing a sense of community and shared purpose.

As months passed, the culture began to shift. Employees felt more valued and engaged, knowing their efforts were recognized and appreciated. Acknowledging small positives built psychological momentum, driving higher morale and greater productivity.

Innovation flourished as team members felt more confident and supported in their roles.

Emily's approach had far-reaching effects beyond immediate productivity gains. The culture of appreciation and mindfulness permeated every level of the organization. Employees began to take pride in their work and in recognizing the efforts of their peers. The positive atmosphere attracted top talent, eager to join a company known for its supportive and appreciative culture.

The company's improved morale and productivity did not go unnoticed by clients and partners. Ideal Moulds Inc.'s reputation as a mindful and forward-thinking company led to new business opportunities and partnerships, further driving its success.

Years later, as Emily reflected on her journey with Master Li, she realized the profound impact of appreciating the small, positive things. She transformed the company into a thriving, innovative, and supportive workplace by scheduling time in her daily routine to acknowledge and celebrate these moments.

The Discipline of Change: How Leadership Transformed Precision Equipment Co.(PEC Inc.)

PEC, a promising startup in the equipment design and manufacturing sector, had grown rapidly in its first few years. However, the company's rapid expansion brought significant challenges. The workplace was chaotic, deadlines were frequently missed, and projects often ran over budget.

Employee burnout was high, and morale was low. The company's culture was one of urgency and disarray, lacking structure and discipline.

Recognizing the need for change, the board of directors brought in Alex Morgan, a leader known for his ability to instill discipline and order in turbulent environments, as the new CEO.

Upon taking the helm, Alex conducted a thorough assessment of PEC's operations and culture. He found that while the team was talented and passionate, there was a severe lack of organizational discipline. Processes were either poorly defined or not followed, and there was little accountability for missed deadlines or budget overruns.

Alex understood that even the most innovative ideas could falter without discipline. He knew that transforming the company's culture required a systematic approach and a commitment to instilling disciplined practices throughout the organization.

Alex began by setting clear expectations and establishing structured processes. He introduced project management frameworks that emphasized planning, execution, and accountability. Each project had defined milestones, and progress was regularly reviewed.

To instill a sense of accountability, Alex implemented performance metrics and regular feedback sessions. He made it clear that meeting deadlines and staying within budget were non-negotiable. However, he also provided the necessary support and resources to help teams succeed, ensuring that discipline was seen as a means to empower rather than constrain.

Alex also focused on building a culture of continuous improvement. He encouraged teams to review their processes regularly, identify areas for improvement, and implement changes. This approach fostered a mindset of disciplined innovation, where creativity was balanced with rigor and execution.

Alex knew that for discipline to take root, he needed to lead by example. He adhered to the same standards he set for his team, demonstrating punctuality, meticulous planning, and a strong work ethic. His consistent behavior reinforced the importance of discipline and showed that it was integral to the company's success.

One pivotal change was Alex's approach to meetings. He ensured that all meetings had clear agendas, started on time, and ended on time. This practice not only improved efficiency but also showed respect for everyone's time, further embedding a culture of discipline.

Over time, the disciplined approach began to pay off. Projects were completed on schedule and within budget, and the quality improved. Employees, initially resistant to the changes, began to appreciate the predictability and structure that discipline brought. They found that a well-organized environment reduced stress and allowed them to focus more on innovation and creativity.

The company's improved performance also had a positive impact on morale. As employees experienced the benefits of a disciplined approach, their confidence in the company's leadership and direction grew. PEC's reputation for reliability and quality in equipment manufacturing strengthened, attracting new clients and investors.

Within two years, PEC had transformed from a chaotic startup into a well-oiled machine. The disciplined culture not only improved operational efficiency but also fostered a more collaborative and innovative environment. Employee satisfaction and retention rates increased, and the company's financial performance saw significant improvements.

Alex's disciplined leadership created a sustainable foundation for growth. Its success story became a model for other startups facing similar challenges, demonstrating that discipline and structure could coexist with creativity and innovation.

Alex Morgan's tenure at PEC highlighted the critical role of discipline in shaping organizational culture. By embedding disciplined practices into the company's DNA, he showed that discipline was not about rigidity but about creating a framework for consistent performance and continuous improvement.

The company continued to thrive under Alex's leadership, and his legacy of disciplined innovation inspired future leaders to embrace structure and accountability as essential components of successful leadership.

Through his disciplined approach, Alex Morgan transformed a company and left an enduring impact on the industry.

In the end, the story of PEC illustrated that with disciplined leadership, even the most dynamic and fast-paced organizations could achieve sustained success and foster a culture where employees could thrive.

The Daily Discipline of Leadership: A Story of Transformation at SteelForge Systems

John Reynolds, the CEO of SteelForge Systems, a leading equipment manufacturer, was known for his visionary thinking and charismatic leadership.

However, as the company grew, John found it increasingly challenging to maintain a clear understanding of how his team was working towards their goals. Despite frequent meetings and reports, he felt disconnected from the day-to-day operations and the challenges his team faced.

Determined to bridge this gap, John decided to develop a disciplined approach to leadership, one that would provide him with clarity and enable him to support his team more effectively.

The Routine: John began by establishing a daily morning ritual. He set his alarm for 5 AM, dedicating the first hour of his day to reflection and planning. He started with a 20-minute meditation session to clear his mind and focus on the present moment. This practice helped him gain mental clarity and reduce stress.

After meditating, John spent 20 minutes journaling. He wrote down his thoughts, goals, and any challenges he anticipated for the day. This exercise allowed him to articulate his priorities and reflect on the broader vision for SteelForge Systems. It also helped him identify potential obstacles that his team might face.

The final 20 minutes of his morning routine were dedicated to physical exercise. Whether it was a brisk jog, a session at the gym, or some yoga, this activity energized him and prepared him for the day ahead. John found that this balanced approach of mind, body, and spirit set a positive tone for his entire day.

Once he arrived at the office, John made it a point to connect with his team members individually. He scheduled short, informal check-ins with key leaders and frontline employees. These conversations were not about micromanaging but about understanding their progress, listening to their concerns, and offering support.

John asked open-ended questions like, "What's going well this week?" and "Are there any obstacles you're facing?" These interactions provided him with valuable insights into the team's morale, the progress of various projects, and any emerging issues. More importantly, they built trust and showed his team that he genuinely cared about their well-being and success.

Through these check-ins, John identified several barriers that were hindering his team's progress. One recurring issue was the inefficiency of the current project management system, which led to miscommunication and delays. Another issue was the lack of cross-departmental collaboration, causing siloed efforts and duplicated work.

John took decisive action to address these issues. He initiated a search for a more intuitive and collaborative project management tool and involved team members in the selection process to ensure it met their needs. He also organized regular cross-departmental meetings to foster collaboration and knowledge sharing. By removing these barriers, John empowered his team to work more efficiently and cohesively.

John's disciplined approach didn't stop at the morning routine and check-ins. He is committed to continuous learning and improvement. He attended leadership workshops, read extensively on management practices, and sought feedback from his team on his performance. He encouraged a culture of continuous improvement within SteelForge Systems, where everyone was motivated to learn and grow.

John's efforts led to a noticeable transformation at SteelForge Systems. Employee morale improved, projects were completed on time, and the company saw a surge in innovation and productivity. The new project management system streamlined workflows, and the regular cross-departmental meetings broke down silos, leading to more cohesive and effective teamwork.

John's disciplined leadership style became a model for others in the industry. His story demonstrated that self-discipline and daily rituals could significantly enhance a leader's ability to understand and support their team. By developing a structured routine, maintaining open communication, and proactively removing barriers, leaders could create an environment where teams thrived, and organizational goals were achieved more efficiently.

Years later, as John looked back on his journey, he realized that the discipline he cultivated not only improved his leadership but also left a lasting impact on SteelForge Systems. The company continued to thrive, driven by a culture of clarity, support, and continuous improvement.

John Reynolds had shown that the power of disciplined leadership could transform not just a company but also the lives of those within it, paving the way for sustained success and fulfillment.

The Spiritual Leader and the Corporate CEO: A Story of Discipline and Transformation

Samantha Lee, the CEO of Machine Works, a cutting-edge manufacturing company, was feeling overwhelmed. Despite her company's success, she struggled with maintaining discipline and focus among her employees. Productivity was declining, and the work culture was becoming increasingly chaotic. Desperate for a solution, she decided to take a break and visit a renowned monastery known for its disciplined way of life.

At the monastery, she met Master Sheng, a wise and serene monk revered for his disciplined lifestyle and profound insights into human behavior. Samantha was intrigued by his calm demeanor and decided to confide in him about her struggles.

Master Sheng listened patiently to Samantha's concerns and then invited her to stay at the monastery for a week to experience their daily routines. Reluctantly, Samantha agreed, hoping to find some answers.

The next morning, Samantha was awakened at 4:30 AM by the sound of a gong. She joined the monks for meditation, followed by a simple breakfast. The rest of the day was structured around study, work, and communal activities, each performed with mindfulness and discipline. Despite the simplicity of their lifestyle, the monks were incredibly focused and content.

Master Sheng explained,

"Discipline is not about rigidly following rules. It's about creating a structure that supports your goals and values.

It's about doing what needs to be done, even when you don't feel like it."

Samantha observed how Master Sheng led by example. He was always the first to rise and the last to rest, demonstrating unwavering commitment to his duties. His actions spoke louder than words, inspiring those around him to follow suit.

Inspired by her experience at the monastery, Samantha returned with a new perspective. She realized that to foster discipline within her organization, she needed to embody it herself.

She began by restructuring her own routine. Samantha started her day early, incorporating meditation and exercise to clear her mind and energize her body. She set specific goals for the day and maintained a disciplined schedule, ensuring she focused on high-priority tasks. Her newfound discipline radiated throughout the company, setting a powerful example for her employees.

She also introduced a series of changes at Machine Works. She established clear expectations and consistent routines, promoting a culture of accountability and mindfulness. Samantha held regular meetings to check in with her team, addressing any obstacles and providing support. She encouraged employees to develop their own daily rituals that aligned with their personal and professional goals.

One pivotal moment came during a major project deadline. The team was under immense pressure, and tensions were high. Instead of succumbing to the stress, Samantha maintained her calm and disciplined approach. Her composed demeanor and structured approach inspired the team to stay focused and work together efficiently.

Samantha's commitment to discipline and mindfulness began to transform the company's culture. Employees started arriving on time, meetings became more productive, and the overall atmosphere improved. The structure and clarity Samantha introduced allowed creativity and innovation to flourish within a framework of disciplined effort.

Over time, the company saw remarkable improvements. Productivity increased, project deadlines were met, and employee satisfaction soared. The company's reputation for disciplined innovation attracted top talent, further driving its success.

Samantha's leadership by example had a profound impact. Her discipline inspired her employees to adopt similar practices, creating a ripple effect throughout the organization. The company became known not just for its technological advancements but also for its positive and disciplined work culture.

Years later, Samantha reflected on her journey. She often visited Master Sheng at the monastery, grateful for the lessons she had learned. Her experience demonstrated that true leadership is about embodying the values you wish to see in your organization.

Samantha Lee had shown that by being a role model for self-discipline, leaders could transform their organizations from the inside out. Her story became an inspiration for other leaders, proving that discipline, mindfulness, and leading by example could create a thriving, successful, and harmonious workplace.

Conclusion

Leadership self-discipline is a cornerstone for transforming the culture of any organization. Leaders who embody self-discipline set the tone for the entire company, creating an environment where discipline becomes a shared value and practice. This transformation begins at the top and cascades down, influencing behaviors, attitudes, and, ultimately, the overall success of the organization.

Self-disciplined leaders establish clear, consistent expectations and follow through on their commitments. This clarity provides a reliable framework within which employees can operate, reducing uncertainty and aligning efforts toward common goals. When leaders consistently model discipline in their actions—arriving on time, meeting deadlines, and adhering to company values—they set a powerful example that inspires employees to adopt similar behaviors.

A disciplined approach to leadership fosters a culture of trust and accountability. Leaders who practice self-discipline demonstrate reliability and integrity, earning the trust of their teams. This trust creates a safe environment where employees feel accountable not only to their leaders but also to each other. When everyone understands that their contributions are valued and that they are expected to deliver consistently, a culture of mutual accountability emerges, enhancing overall performance.

Self-discipline helps leaders prioritize effectively, ensuring that the most critical tasks receive attention and resources. This focus on priorities helps prevent distractions and promotes efficient use of time and energy. When leaders model this behavior, it encourages employees to adopt similar practices, leading to increased productivity and more effective execution of strategic initiatives.

In essence, leadership self-discipline is a transformative force that can reshape the culture of an organization. By setting clear expectations, building trust and accountability, enhancing focus and productivity, promoting continuous improvement, and fostering a positive work environment, disciplined leaders create a foundation for sustained success and growth. The ripple effects of their disciplined

Happiness

The world's most common habit is worrying!

It is estimated that more than 80% of people in the world spend 80% of their time worrying !!

One of the biggest problems with worrying is that it does not make you take action. This leads to a cumulative effect, and every day, we feel a little worse than the previous day.

The Monk and the Snake

In a small monastery nestled in the mountains, a wise old monk lived. One day, a young novice came to him, visibly distressed and troubled with worry. "Master," the novice began, "I am constantly anxious about the future. What if things go wrong? What if I fail in my duties?"

The old monk, with a gentle smile, led the novice to a secluded spot in the forest where a large snake was lying motionless on the ground.

"Do you see that snake?" the monk asked. "It appears to be dead, doesn't it?"

The novice nodded, unsure of where this was going.

The monk continued, "This snake is actually in the process of shedding its old skin. It's a natural process that must happen for it to grow. But if the snake were to worry about the pain and discomfort of shedding, it might never allow itself to go through this transformation. Instead, it embraces the process, knowing that it will emerge renewed and stronger."

The monk then looked deeply into the novice's eyes and said, "Worrying is like the old skin the snake needs to shed. It does not serve you; it holds you back. Instead of worrying, focus on taking action, however small, to move forward. Only through action can you grow and transform."

From that day forward, the novice practiced letting go of his worries and taking small steps every day to fulfill his duties. He found that as he took action, his anxiety diminished, and he felt more at peace with each passing day.

The Worrying CEO

Jane was the CEO of a rapidly growing tech company. One year, they faced a significant setback when a major product launch failed spectacularly. The company lost millions, and the future seemed uncertain. Jane found herself consumed with worry, which started to affect her decision-making and leadership.

One evening, after another sleepless night, Jane decided to visit her mentor, a retired business leader named Mr. Thompson. She poured out her worries about the company's future and her fears of failure.

Mr. Thompson listened patiently and then said, "Jane, let me tell you a story. During my tenure as CEO, we once faced a crisis that threatened to bankrupt the company. I, too, was paralyzed by worry. One day, my advisor said something that changed my perspective forever: 'Worry is a misuse of the imagination. Instead of imagining failure, use that energy to imagine solutions and take action.'"

He continued, "I realized that worrying was not helping me or the company. So, I started focusing on what actions I could take each day, no matter how small. I reached out to our stakeholders, communicated transparently with our team, and devised a new strategy. Slowly but surely, we turned things around."

Mr. Thompson leaned forward and looked Jane in the eyes. "Worrying doesn't change the outcome; action does. Start by identifying one actionable step you can take today to address the issue. Then, do the same tomorrow and the next day. You'll find that not only does your worry diminish, but you also begin to see a path forward."

Inspired by her mentor's story, Jane returned to her company with renewed focus. She rallied her team, encouraged open communication, and together, they developed a new plan. By taking consistent, focused action, they recovered from the setback and eventually achieved even greater success.

A fundamental truth: worrying, while a natural human response, does not lead to solutions or progress. Whether in the spiritual realm or the corporate world, the key to overcoming worry lies in taking actionable steps.

By focusing on what can be done rather than what might go wrong, individuals can transform their anxiety into productive energy, leading to personal growth and success.

Irish philosophy about "worrying. "

In life, there are only two things to worry about whether you are well or sick.

If you are well, then there is nothing to worry about.

If you are sick, you have only two things to worry about: either you will get well, or you will die.

Again, if you get well, there is nothing to worry about.

If you die, there are only two things to worry about either you will go to heaven or hell.

Again, if you go to heaven, there is nothing to worry about.

But if you go to hell, you'll be so damn busy shaking hands with your friends you won't have time to worry!

Reflective Check-Ins

During my leadership years, I always prioritized mental health for my team. We began every day with what we called the "Morning Circle," a special time dedicated not only to discussing projects and deadlines but also to checking in on each other's emotional well-being.

I started noticing a troubling trend: several team members consistently reported feeling stressed and were often in what we termed the "red zone" of mental health. When I delved deeper into the reasons behind their distress, it turned out that 90% of the time, the root cause was triggered by the behavior and attitudes of others.

I began daily check-ins with each team member and conducted a root-cause analysis. In most cases, the issues were beyond their control. Gradually, they came to understand that there was nothing they could do about them, and they began to feel better over time.

Over the following months, I saw a transformative shift in our Morning Circles. The team began to handle emotional challenges with greater autonomy and supported each other in creating a healthier, more empowering work environment.

This experience not only strengthened our team but also reinforced my belief that true leadership involves nurturing a culture where everyone can thrive emotionally and professionally. It was a profound journey that reshaped our office into a community where every individual felt valued and empowered.

A spiritual leader named Gaur Gopal Das has offered an intriguing perspective on worry.

"Why Worry?"

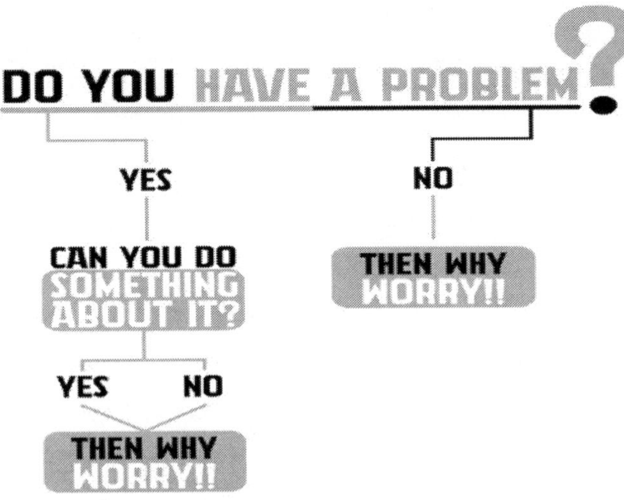

The above visual representation encourages reflection and highlights that there are numerous aspects of life beyond our control, which are both normal and acceptable. Therefore, let's concentrate on the things we can influence or manage.

Personal Strategy which works ..almost always !!

I have a straightforward method to manage worry. When I'm upset, I take a moment to think about the situation.

If my actions have affected others, I let myself feel the consequences and work on a plan to avoid repeating the mistake. I always apologize to anyone involved.

If I'm not the cause of the problem, I simply let it go and move on.

Adopting this practice isn't easy; it takes years of consistent effort to make it a habit.

"A Breath of Fresh Air: Balloons and the Art of Leadership"

In a brightly lit conference room, a diverse group of individuals gathered, each from different walks of life, brought together for a seminar aimed at fostering personal growth and teamwork. The energy was a mix of curiosity and anticipation as they waited for the session to start.

The speaker, a charismatic figure with a warm smile, handed out balloons to each participant. "Write your name on it," he instructed. Each person took a moment to scribble their name on a balloon, infusing a bit of their personality into the bright latex. The balloons were then collected and placed in an adjacent room, transforming it into a sea of floating colors.

The participants were instructed to find the balloon with their name on it within five minutes. As soon as they entered the room, a chaotic ballet ensued. There was shoving and stretching, laughter and shouts—a whirlwind of motion and emotion. Yet, when the time was up, not a single person had found their own balloon.

Sensing their frustration mixed with the lingering adrenaline, the speaker called them back to order. "Now, take the balloon closest to you and look at the name," he said calmly. "Once you find it, give it to the person whose name is written on it."

Within moments, the room shifted from chaos to collaboration. Balloons started floating toward their owners and smiles lit up the room as everyone effortlessly received their named balloon.

The speaker's voice brought home the moral of their experience: "This exercise reveals a profound truth about happiness. Many of us spend our lives frantically searching for our happiness, often in a self-centered scramble. Yet, what this exercise shows is that our happiness often lies in helping others find theirs. When we focus on bringing joy to others, our happiness finds its way back to us."

As the participants left the room, they carried not just their balloons but a new perspective on happiness, contemplating how they might apply this lesson beyond the seminar in the larger balloon-filled room of life.

The power of No Complaining !!

As a leader, I once decided to conduct an experiment with my team that emphasized the power of positivity. The challenge was straightforward but demanding: we all agreed to refrain from any form of complaining for a full week.

This no-complaint rule was to be applied in all contexts—during meetings, casual conversations in the cafeteria, workshops, daily performance reviews, and even in our personal lives with family and friends.

The first two days were the hardest as everyone adjusted to this new mindset. However, by the third day, we began to see a transformative shift.

For the remaining five days, the atmosphere among the team was noticeably different.

This experiment ended up being a profound turning point for us. Not only did it enhance our mental well-being, but it also infused an extraordinary amount of positive energy into our work environment. Remarkably, this change was so palpable that even our internal customers—who were unaware of our internal challenge—noticed a significant positive difference in their interactions with us.

The week came to an end, and while we technically could have reverted to our occasional complaining, the effects of those days without complaints remained with us.

The team didn't just go through a temporary change; there was a deep, meaningful shift in how we viewed ourselves and our work. The positive energy brought about by merely altering ourselves led to remarkable improvements in our activities and notably higher satisfaction among our customers.

This experience highlighted an important lesson: meaningful change starts from within. By deciding not to allow uncontrollable external factors to govern our thoughts and feelings, we found a powerful new approach to shaping our reality and creating a lasting, positive effect in our personal and professional lives.

One of the primary purposes of life is to be happy.

Every human being or species in this world has the right to be happy;

happiness is everybody's birthright, and it should not be linked to any specific achievement.

Monk's Emotional Baggage

Long ago, there was a story about two Buddhist monks, a senior and a junior, traveling together. When they reached a river that they needed to cross, they encountered a young woman who was unsure how to get across.

The junior monk ignored her and crossed the river, but the senior monk chose to help by carrying her across his shoulders. After they continued their journey, the senior monk noticed the junior monk seemed troubled and asked him about his concerns.

The junior monk expressed his unease about the senior monk touching the woman, which was against their monastic rules.

The senior monk explained that although he had indeed helped her, he had left her behind at the river bank and moved on without giving it more thought. He pointed out that while he had physically carried the woman, the junior monk was still mentally carrying the incident, burdened by what had happened even though it was already in the past.

The senior monk emphasized that he had let go of the event as soon as it was over, unlike the junior monk, who continued to carry the emotional weight of the situation.

Alex and his error burden

The founder and CEO of a fast-growing tech startup, Silvia, faced an internal crisis. The company had recently released a software update that, despite thorough testing, contained a significant bug affecting many users. The public backlash was severe, and the development team was demoralized, particularly a talented but inexperienced programmer, Alex, who was responsible for the error.

Silvia convened an emergency meeting with her team. She acknowledged the mistake and the pressure it placed on everyone, especially Alex. Instead of dwelling on the failure, she proposed an aggressive plan to fix the issue and upgrade the customer support response to manage user complaints more effectively.

After the meeting, Silvia noticed Alex seemed unable to move past his mistake, consumed by guilt and anxiety over the consequences of his error. Drawing him aside, Silvia shared the story about two monks she had read, emphasizing the message of letting go of past mistakes. She explained that, like the senior monk who helped someone in need and moved on, they, too, needed to focus on current actions and future solutions rather than past errors.

Inspired by the story, Alex refocused his energy, leading the effort to correct the bug and develop new protocols to prevent similar issues in the future. The successful resolution and subsequent improvements in the software not only restored the company's reputation but also bolstered the team's resilience and unity.

Through this experience, Silvia reinforced a crucial leadership lesson within her startup: the importance of addressing mistakes head-on and moving forward without carrying the burden of past errors.

The Tale of the Lotus Flower

In ancient folklore, there's a captivating tale of a lotus flower blossoming in shadowy, murky waters. Unmarred by the mud, the lotus emerged radiantly pure and stunning, becoming a symbol of resilience and unwavering positivity in the face of adversity.

One serene morning, a wise monk wandering in contemplation came upon this extraordinary flower. Struck by its untouched beauty amidst the gloom, he paused, absorbing its profound symbolism. The lotus whispered a powerful lesson to him: no matter the harshness of our surroundings, we have the choice to foster positivity and maintain the purity of our spirit.

Deeply moved by this revelation, the monk dedicated himself to sharing the lotus's story far and wide. His teachings illuminated minds, showing countless others that even in the darkest corners, inner peace and positivity can not only survive but truly flourish.

The Radiant Startup in the Murky Corporate World

In the bustling landscape of modern business, there's an inspiring tale of a small startup that emerged as a beacon of innovation and resilience. Nestled within the competitive, often ruthless corporate world, this startup, named "Radiant Tech," managed to thrive despite the challenges and pressures surrounding it.

Radiant Tech began in a cramped garage with a handful of passionate individuals who believed in their vision of creating sustainable and eco-friendly technologies. The corporate waters they navigated were murky, with unethical practices, cutthroat competition, and a pervasive focus on profit over purpose. Despite these adverse conditions, Radiant Tech remained steadfast in its mission, never compromising on its values.

One early dawn, the company's CEO, a young and visionary leader named Alex, stood before their modest headquarters. Watching the sunrise, Alex reflected on the journey so far. Radiant Tech had faced numerous setbacks, from funding difficulties to market rejections. Yet, like a lotus blooming in muddy waters, the company had emerged with its core values intact and a growing reputation for integrity and innovation.

Inspired by this quiet moment of clarity, Alex gathered the team for a heartfelt meeting. Alex shared the story of the lotus flower, drawing a parallel to their journey. "Just as the lotus remains pure and beautiful despite its surroundings," Alex said, "we too can rise above the challenges and negativity around us. Our resilience and commitment to our principles are what set us apart."

Motivated by this powerful metaphor, the team redoubled their efforts. They developed groundbreaking products that not only met high environmental standards but also set new benchmarks for the industry. Radiant Tech's unwavering positivity and ethical stance began to attract attention. Investors who valued sustainable growth started showing interest, and partnerships with like-minded companies flourished.

As Radiant Tech's influence grew, Alex became a sought-after speaker, sharing their story of resilience and integrity at various conferences and seminars. Alex's message was clear: in the darkest corners of the business world, it is possible to maintain purity of purpose and foster positivity. Radiant Tech's success became a testament to the power of unwavering commitment to one's values.

The story of Radiant Tech resonated with many, inspiring other startups and established companies alike to reevaluate their practices and embrace a more ethical and sustainable approach. Alex's teachings illuminated minds across the industry, proving that even in the most challenging environments, inner peace and a positive spirit could not only survive but truly flourish.

Conclusion

The relationship between happiness and leadership is profoundly intertwined, especially when it comes to the concept of helping people "let go." Effective leadership plays a pivotal role in fostering an environment where individuals can achieve a sense of fulfillment and well-being.

Leadership that promotes happiness focuses on creating a supportive and empathetic atmosphere where employees feel valued and understood. This involves recognizing the personal and professional burdens that employees carry and helping them navigate these challenges through open communication, appropriate resources, and emotional support.

One key aspect of leadership in this context is the ability to guide individuals in "letting go" of negative emotions, unproductive practices, or past failures. This process is essential for personal growth and development; by encouraging a culture of forgiveness and resilience, leaders can help their teams overcome setbacks and maintain focus on their goals and personal well-being. Moreover, leaders who prioritize happiness often adopt a transformational style in managing their teams through motivation and shared vision; they invest in the development of their people not just in terms of skills and knowledge but also in emotional intelligence and adaptability. This holistic approach not only enhances productivity but also boosts morale and job satisfaction.

In summary, leaders who are adept at supporting their people in letting contribute significantly to a happier, more productive workplace. Such leadership not only improves individuals' well-being but also drives collective success by fostering an environment where everyone feels encouraged to develop their potential.

Reflections

The capacity of humans to exercise introspection and the willingness to learn about their fundamental nature, purpose, and essence.

"Echoes from the Mountain: A Monk's Journey to Enlightened Leadership"

In the tranquil mountains of Bhutan, nestled between clouds and ancient pines, lay the monastery of Sangye Dzong, a bastion of peace and spiritual wisdom. It was here that the young monk, Tashi, embarked on an unexpected journey of leadership that tested his spirit and understanding of the monastic life.

Tashi was just a novice, but his clear voice during chants and his composed demeanor during meditation had already marked him as a future leader among the monks. When the aging abbot, Lama Dorje, noticed Tashi's potential, he decided to prepare him for a leadership role much earlier than usual.

One day, Lama Dorje called Tashi to his modest quarters, filled with the scent of juniper incense and the soft rustle of prayer flags. "Tashi," the old Lama began, "leadership in our tradition is not just about guiding others forward; it's about understanding the steps we have taken before. This understanding will be your first true test."

Tashi listened intently as Lama Dorje shared a plan that both excited and terrified him. He was to embark on a solitary retreat in the ancient cave of Milarepa, high above the monastery. This retreat was traditionally reserved for senior monks to reflect on their past actions and seek insights into their spiritual journey.

As Tashi ascended the mountain path to the cave, he felt the weight of his new responsibility. He spent days and nights in solitude, with only a small painting of Milarepa for company. The isolation was profound, forcing Tashi to confront his past actions, his doubts, and his aspirations. The journey of leadership, he realized, was indeed not a constant forward motion but a deep, reflective pause that allowed him to reconnect with his purpose.

After a month in solitude, Tashi returned to the monastery. He was visibly changed, his eyes deeper and his presence calmer. Lama Dorje greeted him with a knowing smile. "What have you learned, young leader?" he asked.

Tashi shared his insights, his voice resonant with newfound wisdom.

"To lead is to serve, and to serve effectively, we must understand our own journey. We must pause to reflect on each step, not just to see where it has taken us but to understand why we took it in the first place."

Lama Dorje nodded in approval, and from that day on, Tashi took on more responsibilities at the monastery. His leadership style was marked by periods of action interspersed with moments of reflection, inspiring other monks to adopt a more contemplative approach to their roles.

Tashi's story spread beyond Sangye Dzong, becoming a lesson in leadership and self-reflection. It reminded everyone that true progress often requires us to stop, look back, and learn from the path we have traveled. This insight, born from the silence of a mountain cave, illuminated not just his journey but the paths of those he led.

Reflect to Innovate: The Transformation of Leadership at MovaLink Solutions"

In a bustling city at the heart of Silicon Valley stood the innovative tech startup MovaLink, known for its cutting-edge software solutions and dynamic corporate culture. Elena, the company's CEO, was a visionary leader whose rapid rise to the top was marked by aggressive growth and technological breakthroughs. However, she soon faced a leadership crisis that challenged the very foundations of her approach to management and growth.

Elena had always prioritized fast scaling and innovation, but the rapid expansion brought unforeseen challenges. The company began experiencing severe burnout among employees, project delays, and a decline in product quality. The board of directors expressed concern about the company's direction and sustainability, prompting Elena to reconsider her leadership strategy.

Reflecting on the mantra that "The journey of leadership is not just forward motion; it's also the ability to pause and reflect on past steps," Elena decided to initiate a company-wide reflective retreat. The objective was clear: to pause the relentless pursuit of progress and instead reflect on the company's journey, evaluate its current practices, and realign its goals.

The retreat took place in a serene location outside the city, away from the usual hustle of tech life. It included workshops, team-building activities, and sessions dedicated to open discussions about the company's processes, culture, and future. Elena encouraged everyone to share their experiences and insights, highlighting the importance of each voice in shaping the company's path forward.

During these sessions, Elena listened intently to the feedback about the need for more sustainable work practices, better communication channels, and a greater focus on employee well-being. It became clear that while her forward-thinking vision was crucial, it needed to be balanced with introspection and consideration for the team's well-being.

Armed with these insights, Elena returned to the office with a new leadership approach. She implemented changes that included flexible working hours, transparent communication policies, and a new project management framework that allowed for more downtime and creative freedom.

Elena also scheduled quarterly reflection retreats to ensure the company continuously aligned its practices with its core values and employee needs.

These changes significantly transformed the company culture. Employee satisfaction soared, innovation flourished in a more supportive environment, and the company stabilized its growth with renewed focus and vigor.

Elena's story became a celebrated example in business circles. It illustrated that true leadership involves not just pushing forward but also knowing when to pause and reflect. It highlighted a modern approach to leadership that values both progress and introspection, leading to a more balanced and sustainable path forward.

"Reflections of Dedication: A Gardener's Clever Test"

A young man made a phone call from a public booth to a woman, asking if she needed someone to mow her lawn. She informed him that she already employed someone for that service. Persisting, he suggested he could do the job for half the price, but she was content with her current gardener and declined.

Not giving up, he then offered to clean her house and stairs for free and mow the lawn at a discounted rate. She refused again and ended the call. The owner of the phone booth, who had listened to the entire exchange, felt for the young man and offered him employment at his store.

Surprisingly, the young man declined, revealing with a grin that he was, in fact, the woman's gardener, just checking whether she was satisfied with his work. The booth owner admired the young man's dedication to his job and recognized that such commitment could indeed lead to favorable results.

The Japanese translation for self-reflection: Hansei.

When a Japanese child errs, their parents instruct them to engage in "Hansen." This request implies that the child should feel remorse and enhance their demeanor, encompassing both spirit and attitude. Thus, the child clearly understands what the parents expect when they are told to perform handsets.

Hansei involves an intentional process of introspection. During this process, one assesses what aspects went well and which did not and commits to improving in the future.

Hansei goes beyond mere reflection; it entails a deep honesty about one's shortcomings. While discussing only our strengths might come off as boastful, acknowledging our weaknesses sincerely demonstrates considerable strength.

Hansei involves three crucial elements:

First, the individual must acknowledge a discrepancy between what was expected and what was achieved, always remaining receptive to critical feedback, regardless of the source's rank or status.

Secondly, the individual should willingly accept personal responsibility and experience profound remorse. This aspect of Hansei is emotionally intense.

Lastly and most critically, the individual must pledge to undertake personal actions and commit to a definite plan to improve themselves. Recognizing an issue and feeling regret without subsequent action renders the process futile and merely a waste of time.

The Enlightened CEO

In the spiritual world and modern leadership, the story of Anna, a tech company CEO, exemplifies the power of Hansei. Anna's company was thriving, yet employee satisfaction scores were consistently low. Realizing there was a significant gap between her leadership style and employee expectations, Anna embraced the principle of Hansei.

First, she acknowledged the problem during a company-wide meeting, openly inviting feedback from all levels of the organization. This step was difficult, as it exposed her to a barrage of critical feedback about her management approach, which many found to be too distant and demanding.

Taking personal responsibility, Anna expressed deep regret for any stress or dissatisfaction her leadership style had caused. Her heartfelt apology set the stage for genuine change, marking the emotional cornerstone of her Hansei.

Determined to lead differently, Anna committed to specific actions: she initiated monthly town hall meetings to foster open communication, participated in leadership coaching to enhance her empathy and engagement skills, and set up a task force to regularly assess the impact of the new measures.

Over time, employee satisfaction dramatically improved, and Anna's company not only retained its competitive edge but also became renowned for its positive workplace culture. Anna's story is a testament to how the principles of Hansei can lead to transformative outcomes in both spiritual growth and effective modern leadership.

"Ubuntu: Embracing Humanity Through Community Forgiveness"

In some parts of South Africa, when someone commits an error, they are brought to the village center and encircled by their tribe for two days. During this time, tribe members recount all the positive actions the individual has performed.

This stems from the belief that everyone is inherently good but occasionally makes mistakes as a plea for help. Through this ritual, the community comes together to help the individual remember their true self. They believe that solidarity and positive reinforcement are more effective for changing behavior than shame and punishment.

This philosophy is referred to as ubuntu, which means humanity towards others.

"Unity in Crisis: Embracing Ubuntu in Modern Leadership"

In the realm of modern leadership, the philosophy of ubuntu—emphasizing humanity towards others—was poignantly illustrated by the actions of a corporate CEO of a multinational tech company. The story begins when the company faced a severe crisis due to a significant software failure that affected millions of users globally. The failure not only caused widespread disruption but also threatened the company's reputation and stock value.

The CEO, instead of resorting to the traditional approach of assigning blame and penalizing the team responsible, chose to embrace the principles of ubuntu. She called for an all-hands meeting, not to chastise but to unify and heal. During the meeting, she acknowledged the pressure and hard work of her teams and highlighted numerous instances where employees had demonstrated exceptional dedication and innovation. She expressed her belief that every team member inherently aimed to contribute positively and that the crisis was a collective setback rather than an individual failure.

Following the principles of ubuntu, she initiated a "restorative circle," similar to the tribal gatherings in South Africa. In this circle, each member of the crisis management team shared their experiences and learnings from the incident. Instead of hiding their mistakes, they were encouraged to bring them to light without fear of reprisal. The CEO affirmed each contribution and focused on the collective wisdom gained rather than the errors made.

This approach not only boosted morale but also fostered a culture of openness, trust, and mutual support. Employees were motivated to collaborate more closely, share their knowledge, and innovate solutions to prevent future crises. The company emerged stronger and more cohesive.

The CEO's use of Ubuntu was transformative, reinforcing that leadership grounded in empathy, community, and the recognition of shared humanity can lead to more resilient and innovative organizations. Her leadership during the crisis became a case study at business schools. It was featured in several leadership seminars, highlighting the power of positive reinforcement over punishment in modern corporate management.

No matter how good I am, there is always somebody somewhere who is better than me.

Once, in a small mountain village known for its serene beauty and spiritual tranquility, lived an elderly sage named Ananda. For decades, Ananda was revered as the wisest elder in the village, known for his profound spiritual insights and gentle guidance. He had led the village through countless hardships with a calm and steady hand, earning him the respect and love of all the villagers.

One day, a young woman named Mira arrived in the village. She was a traveler from a distant land, seeking wisdom and enlightenment. Mira had a natural charisma and an undeniable sense of leadership that quickly caught the attention of the villagers.

As she settled into village life, she began to share her own fresh and deeply insightful insights, which resonated with the younger generation. Her presence sparked a new energy in the village, and soon, people began to turn to her for guidance as much as they did to Ananda.

At first, Ananda felt a prick of unease. He had always been the sole beacon of wisdom in the village, and Mira's presence challenged the role he had played for so many years. However, he remembered a mantra he had often recited but seldom had the chance to embody: "No matter how good I am, there is always somebody somewhere who is better than me." This humbling thought brought him a sense of peace.

Instead of seeing Mira as a threat, Ananda saw her as an opportunity for his growth and the enrichment of the village. He began to collaborate with Mira, blending the old ways with her new perspectives. This partnership brought about a renaissance of sorts in the village, combining Ananda's deep, traditional wisdom with Mira's innovative ideas and vibrant energy.

The villagers, old and young, benefited immensely from this union of minds. The younger generation felt more connected to the village's spiritual roots, while the older residents found new excitement in Mira's fresh approaches. Together, Ananda and Mira demonstrated that true leadership is not about maintaining status or fearing change but about embracing growth and recognizing that leadership can come from anywhere and anyone.

Their story became a legend in the village. It was a tale of humility, partnership, and the continuous journey of learning. It taught that every leader, no matter how experienced or revered, has something to learn from others and that the true essence of wisdom lies in the openness to continually evolve.

"Driving Excellence: Toyota's Reflective Approach"

Toyota demonstrates a prime illustration of individual and team reflection. When Toyota launched the highly successful Avalon model in the 1990s, it was an immediate bestseller.

Despite this success, the project team didn't just bask in their achievement; instead, they quickly convened to discuss what could have been better in the car's development and manufacturing processes. Even with the model's great success, they identified numerous areas for improvement and shared these insights with other teams.

Toyota's distinct behaviors and practices, markedly different from those of its competitors, played a crucial role in maintaining its competitive edge. This approach epitomizes its corporate culture.

A Story from the Zen Monastery to the Boardroom

In the tranquil hills of Japan, nestled among blossoming cherry trees, was a small Zen monastery known for its profound spiritual teachings and the cultivation of deep self-awareness among its monks. The monastery was led by Master Kaito, whose wisdom was revered far and wide. His teachings often transcended the confines of the spiritual and ventured into the practical realms of daily living and leadership.

Master Kaito's approach was not just about inner peace but also about continuous improvement, a principle he encapsulated with a simple phrase, *kaizen*, which means 'change for the better.' This concept was deeply ingrained in every monk who trained under him, emphasizing that enlightenment was a journey, not a destination.

This perspective taught the monks to constantly reflect on their actions and thoughts, seeking improvement even in seemingly perfect situations.

Several kilometers away, in the bustling city center, stood the headquarters of a major corporation struggling to keep up with the competitive market. The company, once a leader in innovation, had grown complacent with its past successes.

Observing this, one of the board members, Naomi, proposed a radical idea. Naomi, a former student of Master Kaito, suggested implementing the *kaizen* philosophy at the corporate level, inspired by her time at the monastery.

Naomi shared a compelling story with her fellow executives—a story about the monks of her old monastery. She described how after a day of what seemed like perfect meditation and chores, the monks would gather under the old ginkgo tree to discuss what could have been done better. This reflection was not a critique but a humble acknowledgment that improvement was always possible and necessary.

Inspired by this story, the company decided to shift its culture. They started by examining their most successful project to date, akin to Toyota's reflection on the Avalon model. Instead of celebrating the project's success at face value, the leadership team met to dissect what could have been done better. This reflection was not a sign of dissatisfaction but a commitment to continuous improvement.

The new approach was transformative. Like the monks' reflections under the ginkgo tree, the company's regular review meetings became a source of powerful insights and innovative ideas, propelling them back to a leadership position in the industry. The employees, now engaged in a culture that valued their input and fostered personal and professional growth, felt more aligned and committed to the company's vision.

Naomi's integration of Master Kaito's spiritual teachings into modern corporate leadership not only revived a struggling company but also created a thriving culture where continuous improvement became the cornerstone of success. Just as the monks at the monastery sought spiritual enlightenment, the company pursued excellence in every endeavor, proving that the principles of spiritual growth and modern leadership could indeed harmonize to create extraordinary results.

Conclusion

Reflecting on leadership practices is not just an exercise in self-improvement but a pivotal action that shapes the entire cultural fabric of an organization. Through leadership reflections, leaders gain valuable insights into their own behaviors, decision-making processes, and interaction styles.

This self-awareness allows them to adapt and refine their approaches, which is crucial in fostering a positive, innovative, and responsive organizational culture.

Moreover, when leaders demonstrate a commitment to reflection and personal growth, they set a powerful example for all members of the organization, promoting a culture of continuous learning and openness to change.

This environment not only enhances employee engagement and satisfaction but also drives organizational success by aligning personal growth with business objectives.

In essence, leadership reflections catalyze a transformative impact on organizational culture, making it more adaptive, resilient, and aligned with the values and goals of the organization.

EGO

Spirituality in Leadership means letting go of Ego, embracing humility, and leading with a heart open to Serve

---

The Scholar and the Boatman: A Lesson in True Wisdom

A long time ago, a highly educated man was traveling across a river in a boat. During the journey, he started a conversation with the boatman, who appeared uneducated and impoverished. The educated man asked if the boatman was familiar with the Vedas, ancient Indian religious texts. When the boatman confessed he hadn't heard of them, the scholar indignantly claimed the boatman had wasted 25% of his life.

The conversation continued, and the scholar asked about the Upanishads, another set of ancient Hindu scriptures. The boatman's ignorance led the scholar to declare he had wasted 50% of his life. Further questioning about major works of Indian epic literature elicited similar responses, and the scholar concluded that the boatman had wasted his entire life.

However, as they reached the middle of the river, the boat began to leak and take on water, causing panic among the passengers. As people started jumping into the water, the boatman asked the educated man if he could swim. When the scholar admitted he couldn't, the boatman pointed out that despite his vast knowledge of literature and philosophy, it wouldn't save him from drowning.

In life's most critical moments, practical skills and humility often prove far more valuable than theoretical knowledge. True wisdom lies not in what you know but in how you apply it to survive and thrive.

Taoism *views the ego as arising when the human-centric mind becomes unbalanced, excessively focusing on humanity, control, striving to be the best, or seeking perfection.*

Buddhism *describes the ego as "I, me, my" thinking, exemplified by thoughts like "I did this," "Listen to me," or "This is mine."*

As Buddha sought enlightenment and ways to end suffering, he asked himself, "Who is this 'I' within me?" Seeing people in pain and sickness and facing death, he wondered, "Who is this 'I' in you, especially when even our bodies don't truly belong to us?"

The Resurgence of Maya: A Tale of Triumph, Defeat, and Redemption

Maya Jennings was a fiercely ambitious tech entrepreneur in Silicon Valley. She had recently launched a cutting-edge app that used artificial intelligence to personalize education for children. As the app gained popularity, so did Maya's reputation. Her every sentence seemed to start with "I did this" or "My team followed my vision." She believed fiercely in the power of her genius, often overshadowing the collaborative efforts of her diverse team.

As her success grew, so did Maya's ego. She surrounded herself with yes-men and women who echoed her beliefs and praised her every decision. Her social media profiles became a constant stream of self-promotion and self-congratulation, emphasizing her sole influence on her company's success. "Listen to me," she'd begin in meetings, her tone more dismissive over time as she increasingly ignored dissenting opinions.

However, the tech world is fickle. When a major software bug caused a privacy breach, the same voices that had praised Maya turned against her. Investors pulled back, users deleted the app, and her company's value plummeted. Yet, Maya's initial reactions were still tinged with denial and self-importance. "This is my company; I will fix everything," she declared, unwilling to acknowledge the magnitude of the problem or the cooperative effort needed to resolve it.

It was during this crisis that Maya encountered Buddhism through a mindfulness retreat recommended by a former mentor. Here, she was introduced to the concept of the ego as "I, me, my" thinking. The lessons were clear and pointed directly at her failings—her attachment to self-identity and personal achievement had blinded her to the collective nature of success and the impermanence of all things.

Slowly, Maya began to change. She returned to her company with a new perspective. "We have a problem, but together, we can solve it," she began saying in meetings. She listened more than she spoke, acknowledged her team's contributions, and shared credit. The shift was gradual but profound. Her company began to recover, not just financially but culturally, as a place where every voice mattered.

Years later, Maya's company had not only stabilized but became a leader in ethical AI development. Maya herself became a sought-after speaker, not for her singular vision but for her ability to lead inclusively and humbly. She often shared her journey, highlighting her mistakes driven by ego and the Buddhist teachings that helped reshape her understanding of success.

Maya had learned that "I, me, my" could be transformed into "we, us, ours," strengthening and resiliency in not just her company but also her entire community.

Buddha and Humility

Once upon a time, in the ancient lands where the Buddha lived, a unique event unfolded that would forever echo as a lesson in humility and genuine charity.

One serene morning, the Buddha declared that he would only receive offerings on that day, inviting people from all societal levels to partake in the giving. News of this spread like wildfire, attracting numerous wealthy dignitaries and powerful rulers who seized the opportunity to display their affluence.

They arrived with carts laden with treasures, presenting them to Buddha with great ceremony. However, Buddha received these lavish gifts with a mere single hand, an unusual and seemingly dismissive gesture, given that true acceptance required both hands, symbolizing wholehearted gratitude.

Among the crowd was an elderly woman, frail and bent from the burdens of poverty. She had traveled miles, moved by a sincere desire to offer what little she had. Approaching Buddha, she presented him with half a pomegranate, explaining that it was all she could afford, having consumed the other half to sustain her journey. In stark contrast to his earlier receptions, Buddha stood and accepted her modest gift with both of his hands, treating it with as much reverence as if it were a treasure trove.

This disparity in reception sparked whispers and, eventually, outright indignation among wealthy donors. Unable to contain their displeasure, one confronted Buddha, questioning why he honored such a trivial offering with more respect than their substantial gifts. With a calm that stilled the murmuring crowd, Buddha explained that while their donations were indeed grand, they represented only a fraction of their vast fortunes and were motivated more by vanity than by virtue. The elderly woman, on the other hand, had given everything she could with a heart full of joy and generosity, making her humble gift infinitely more valuable.

Thus, through this simple yet profound act, Buddha taught that the essence of giving lies not in the magnitude of the gift but in the sincerity and purity of the intention behind it. True generosity requires giving selflessly, valuing the act of giving over the gift itself. This lesson resonated deeply, reminding all that the true measure of a gift is the spirit in which it is given, not the material value it holds.

The famous Chinese Tao teachings written by Tao Te Ching more than 2600 years ago states,

"The sage puts himself last and becomes the first."

Water, one of nature's greatest gifts to humanity, serves as an exemplary model of humility. Like supreme goodness, water benefits all without conflict. It remains grounded in its environment, delves deep into its essence, and maintains honesty in its expression. Even in disputes, it is gentle, and it does not exert control when governing. Water's actions are well-timed, and it is at peace with its inherent nature, making it beyond reproach.

As it courses through rivers, the water stays humble, nourishing plants and supporting wildlife without any self-centered intentions. It asks for nothing in return, and life on Earth would be unimaginable without it. Thus, water sets an ideal standard for leadership.

Leaders should look to water as a role model, embodying humility that shifts the focus towards the advancement and triumphs of others rather than their own. This approach not only fosters personal satisfaction but also encourages leaders to facilitate opportunities for others to succeed. The strength of water and leaders alike stems from humility, which empowers them to stay grounded, be present, and learn from others—a lesson in humility from water that all leaders can benefit from.

The Story of Elena Ramirez

A pioneering CEO who transformed her company by embodying the qualities of water—humility, adaptability, and a focus on collective success. Elena took the helm of a struggling tech company known for its cutthroat culture and stagnant innovation. Inspired by the nature of water, she set out to make fundamental changes, not just in strategy but in the ethos of the company's leadership.

Elena introduced her philosophy during her first address to the company, using the metaphor of water to illustrate her vision. She described water's powerful humility—how it nourishes everything it touches without seeking acknowledgment or reward. She shared her belief that leadership, like water, should not dominate but instead help others rise and succeed.

Under Elena's guidance, the company shifted from prioritizing individual achievements to fostering an environment where every team member could thrive. She implemented mentorship programs where experienced employees guided newcomers in developing not just skills but also a mindset focused on collective growth and success.

Elena's leadership style had a profound impact. The company began to innovate at an unprecedented rate because employees felt more connected and valued and were encouraged to share ideas without fear of being overshadowed or disregarded. In meetings, Elena remained grounded and present, actively listening and gently steering discussions to deeper insights and resolutions, much like water shaping the landscape quietly yet powerfully.

Elena also led by example in confronting challenges. When the company faced significant market shifts, she remained calm and adaptable, navigating through these changes with strategic adjustments that seemed to naturally align with the company's needs, mirroring water's effortless alignment with its surroundings.

Under her leadership, the company not only rebounded but flourished, expanding its reach globally and significantly improving employee satisfaction and retention rates. Elena's leadership showed that humility does not mean weakness; rather, it is a strength that propels others forward, fosters a supportive culture, and drives sustainable success.

Through her journey, Elena Ramirez became more than just a CEO; she became a symbol of how embracing the humility and adaptability of water can lead to profound transformations in both leadership and business success. Her story is a testament to the power of leading by nurturing, an approach that turns potential into abundance.

"Silencing the Ego: The Power of Ignoring External Opinions"

The Monk and the Mirror

In ancient Japan, there lived a monk named Akira, who was deeply respected for his wisdom and serenity. Akira resided in a monastery where he taught young acolytes the ways of Zen. One of the central teachings he emphasized was the importance of ignoring the ego and the perceptions others may have.

One evening, during a gathering, a visiting nobleman mockingly asked Akira, "How can you teach about the ego when you are constantly praised? How do you not grow vain?" In response, Akira asked the nobleman to bring a mirror the next day. When the nobleman returned, Akira took the mirror and, looking into it, said, "When I look into this mirror, I see neither a wise man nor a foolish one. The mirror shows only the reflection present at the moment.

Just as the mirror does not cling to the reflection, so I do not cling to any image of myself held by others."

This lesson spread far and wide, illustrating how detaching from one's self-image and the opinions of others is essential to true wisdom.

The Leadership of Alfredo: A Lesson in Ego and Perception

In the heart of a bustling city, Alfredo, the CEO of a prominent manufacturing company, was widely admired for his wisdom and composed nature. Alfredo had built his company from the ground up and was known for his exceptional ability to mentor young professionals. He emphasized the importance of setting aside one's ego and not being influenced by others' opinions.

One day, during a company-wide meeting, a visiting executive mockingly questioned Alfredo, "How can you preach about humility when you receive constant praise? How do you avoid becoming arrogant?" Alfredo responded with a calm smile and asked the executive to bring a clear glass of water the next day.

When the executive returned with the glass of water, Alfredo held it up for everyone to see and said, "When I look at this water, I see neither purity nor impurity. The water merely reflects whatever is put into it."

"Just as this water does not cling to any impurities or purities introduced into it, I do not cling to any image of myself held by others," Alfredo explained.

This simple yet powerful lesson quickly spread throughout the company, highlighting the importance of detaching from one's self-image and the opinions of others. Alfredo's wisdom taught his employees that true leadership and personal growth come from focusing on the present and not being swayed by external validation or criticism.

Under Alfredo's leadership, the manufacturing company thrived, not just in terms of profits but also by fostering a culture of humility and continuous self-improvement. His story inspired leaders within the company and beyond, demonstrating that true leadership lies in the ability to stay grounded and self-aware, regardless of external praise or criticism.

"Silencing the Ego: Never Take Success for Granted"

The Emperor and the Hidden Garden

In ancient China, there lived an emperor named Han Wei, who was known for his military prowess and vast empire. Despite his many conquests, Han Wei sought the counsel of a wise old sage to find lasting peace and happiness. The sage led the emperor to a neglected garden within the imperial grounds and handed him a simple shovel.

"For one year, you must tend to this garden without the help of your servants," instructed the sage. Han Wei, though initially resistant, committed to the task, believing it would teach him a great secret of power.

As the seasons changed, Han Wei labored in the garden, his hands becoming calloused and his back sore. Slowly, the garden transformed from a barren plot to a lush oasis brimming with life. Through this process, Han Wei learned humility and the value of hard work, recognizing that his success as an emperor should not be taken for granted. The garden flourished not because of his title but because of his effort and care.

When the year ended, the sage returned and said, "Like this garden, all success requires continuous nurturing and humility. Do not take your victories for granted, for they need constant care to remain fruitful."

CEO Stephie Thompson and the Factory Turnaround

In the contemporary corporate world, Stephie Thompson rose to the position of CEO at a struggling manufacturing company. Her predecessors had ridden on the waves of past successes, becoming complacent and disconnected from the day-to-day operations that kept the company alive.

Determined to turn the company around, Stephie took a hands-on approach. She spent her first month working alongside employees at every level of the company, from the factory floor to the design team, understanding the intricacies and challenges of each department.

Through her direct involvement, Stephie not only gained valuable insights into operational inefficiencies but also demonstrated to her employees that success is a continuous journey that requires the involvement and dedication of everyone in the organization. Her approach fostered a culture of mutual respect and collaboration, which led to innovative solutions that revived the company's fortunes.

Under Stephie's leadership, the company not only recovered but became a leader in sustainable practices. This shows that, like Han Wei's garden, a company must be diligently cared for and never taken for granted.

"Silencing the Ego: Owning Our Failures Without Blame"

Ancient Spiritual Story: The Archer and the Storm

In ancient India, there lived a renowned archer named Devraj who was famed for his unmatched skill with the bow. People from far and wide would come to witness his prowess at festivals and competitions. However, Devraj's pride grew with his fame, and he began to see himself as infallible.

One stormy day, during a major archery contest, strong winds thwarted Devraj's arrows. Each miss incited jeers from the crowd, and in his embarrassment, Devraj blamed the storm for his failures, claiming it was an unfair disadvantage.

Witnessing this, an old monk approached him and said softly, "True mastery, young archer, lies not in perfect conditions but in adapting to the imperfections of life."

The monk invited Devraj to his serene temple, nestled amidst towering mountains and tranquil streams. There, in the quietude of the temple grounds, the monk began to teach Devraj the profound practice of meditation and the art of inner focus. They would sit together in the early morning mist, the world around them hushed and still, as the monk guided Devraj through deep breathing exercises and mindful contemplation.

The monk instructed Devraj to close his eyes and focus on the rhythm of his breath, to let go of all distractions and immerse himself in the present moment. Through these sessions, Devraj learned to quiet his restless mind and delve deep into his own consciousness. The monk introduced him to ancient techniques that sharpened his concentration, enabling him to maintain unwavering focus even amidst chaos.

As the days turned into weeks, Devraj discovered a newfound clarity and calmness within himself. He began to see his failures not as the fault of external forces but as reflections of his own inner state. The monk's teachings illuminated the path to self-awareness, showing Devraj that true mastery came from within.

This transformative experience went beyond archery; it reshaped Devraj's entire outlook on life. He realized that every setback was a chance to learn and evolve. Embracing this wisdom, Devraj became not only a better archer but also a paragon of humility and resilience.

In time, Devraj's reputation as a wise and skilled archer spread far and wide. He established his own school, where he taught future generations the lessons he had learned at the temple. His teachings emphasized the importance of inner strength, mindfulness, and taking responsibility for one's actions.

Through his guidance, many young archers learned to see challenges as opportunities for growth, embodying the principles of humility and perseverance that Devraj had so deeply internalized.

CEO Laura Becker and the Market Crisis

Laura Becker was the CEO of a burgeoning fintech company, known for her sharp intellect and decisive nature. Under her leadership, the company had seen rapid growth and was on the brink of going public. However, an unexpected financial crisis shook the market, severely impacting her company's performance.

Initially, Laura was quick to blame external factors: market conditions, regulatory changes, and even her team's handling of the situation. However, her mindset began to shift after she attended a leadership seminar where the story of Devraj was discussed in the context of personal accountability.

Inspired by the ancient tale, Laura returned to her company with a new approach. She held a series of meetings in which she openly acknowledged her earlier tendency to blame external factors rather than address internal weaknesses. By embracing her failures, Laura fostered a culture of transparency and continuous improvement within her team.

She initiated a comprehensive review of the company's strategies and encouraged her team to innovate and pivot without fear of blame. This shift not only stabilized the company during turbulent times but also led to a stronger, more cohesive leadership structure.

Laura's experience, much like Devraj's, shows that leadership involves embracing failures as personal learning opportunities rather than deflecting responsibility. Both stories underline a timeless lesson: silencing our ego by owning our mistakes is crucial for personal growth and effective leadership.

I keep my ego in check with a simple daily practice. Every morning when I wake up, I remind myself,

"No matter how skilled I am, someone out there is better."

Conclusion

In concluding this chapter, we have delved into the profound significance of humility and the elimination of ego in leadership. As we've explored through various narratives and teachings, from ancient wisdom to contemporary practices, humility stands not as a sign of weakness but as a cornerstone of true leadership strength. It fosters an environment of growth, learning, and mutual respect among team members.

Leaders who prioritize humility over ego are equipped to build more resilient organizations. They create cultures that are adaptable to change and welcoming of innovation, where ideas can flourish without the constraints of hierarchy or personal pride. Such leaders are not merely administrators but visionaries who inspire loyalty and drive toward collective success.

Ego, on the other hand, can blind leaders to their own faults and isolate them from valuable feedback; it can create barriers within the team and halt progress. Thus, meeting one's ego and cultivating humanity is not just a personal journey but also a strategic imperative for effective leadership.

By integrating the lessons of humanity into their leadership style, leaders can ensure that they remain open to learning and responsive to change, making decisions that benefit stakeholders. The journey of great leadership is continuous and often requires a conscious effort to keep the ego in check. Ensuring that humanity guides our actions and decisions. This approach not only enhances personal character but fundamentally strengthens the very fabric of our organizations.

Conclusion

In my twenty-year journey through the spheres of professional leadership, I have gleaned invaluable insight: beneath the robust facade of leadership skills such as motivation, delegation, and communication lie a deeper, more transformative layer—what I term the "spiritual characteristics" of leadership.

This isn't about religious or mystical connotations but rather a profound alignment with the inner self, a concept I have explored through the spiritual leadership model presented in this book. These characteristics form the bedrock upon which true leadership prowess can be built, and ignoring them can lead to significant shortcomings in organizational transformations.

My realization did not come overnight. It was a gradual awakening punctuated by numerous leadership challenges and reflective moments. For instance, early in my career, I led a team tasked with a pivotal project that was struggling disastrously. Despite applying every conventional leadership tactic, from clear communication to strategic delegation, the project was teetering on the brink of failure.

It was only when I took a step back to analyze not just the strategies but the core motivations and beliefs driving our team's efforts that I understood the disconnect.

This introspection revitalized our approach, primarily by aligning the team's deeper values and purposes with the project's goals. The turnaround was dramatic. This experience was a cornerstone in shaping my belief in the power of spiritual characteristics in leadership.

As I expanded on these insights, I felt a compelling need to share this foundational perspective with other leaders. The conventional literature on leadership is replete with strategies and tips; however, it often glosses over the essence of leadership that emanates from within. True leadership transformation is a journey of internal discovery and alignment, a theme that is central to this book.

This realization prompted me to encourage every leader to write their leadership narrative. While the eight elements of the spiritual leadership model I proposed are derived from my experiences, they may only sometimes apply. Every leader's journey is unique, and understanding one's core values and motivations is crucial. This personalization of leadership is theoretical and practical. As I crafted each chapter, I delved into personal stories and reflections, which not only helped me articulate my thoughts but also solidified my own understanding and commitment to these principles.

Consider the story of a CEO I once coached who struggled with significant turnover at his company. He had tried various incentives and team-building exercises, but nothing seemed to work. Through our sessions, it became apparent that his leadership style, though effective in driving results, did not resonate with the values and needs of his employees. By re-aligning his approach to reflect a more inclusive and empathetic leadership style, one that was true to his own re-discovered values, he was able to reduce turnover and improve morale significantly. This transformation was a direct result of his embrace of the spiritual dimensions of leadership.

The assumption that all senior leaders automatically possess the right mindset for successful transformations needs to be revised and often leads to failures. My own experience and the stories I've encountered underscored the need to address this gap. Initially, I planned to discuss the strategies for successful organizational transformations. Still, I quickly realized that with a solid foundation in the spiritual characteristics of leadership, these strategies would be more effective.

Thus, this book serves as a foundational discourse for my subsequent work, "Spiritual Lean Transformation." It is intended to prepare leaders not just to implement changes but to be the change themselves. This involves a deep, reflective journey into the self, which I hope this book facilitates.

In closing, thank you for joining me on this journey of self-realization and continuous improvement. The path to leadership excellence is both challenging and rewarding, and it requires a steadfast commitment to growth, both personally and professionally.

As you turn the pages of your own leadership journey, remember that the deepest insights often come from within and that true transformation begins in the leader's heart and mind. Let us step forward with the resolve not only to lead but inspire, not just direct but empower, and not just manage but transform..

About the Author

Vetri Janakiraman is a skilled Operational Excellence mentor emphasizing process improvement and people development. His extensive career has transformed multiple organizations in various sectors, including Automotive, Pharma, Industrial Automation, Engineering, Life Sciences, Food and Beverage, and Electrical. Vetri brings a wealth of experience to the field of leadership development. Over the past five years, he has undergone a profound spiritual transformation seamlessly integrated into his professional journey.

Vetri holds a Master's in Operations Management and is a certified John Maxwell trainer and coach. His deep understanding of operational and spiritual dynamics equips him to provide unique insights into leadership.

"Spiritual Leadership Transformation" was inspired when Vetri observed a rising number of leadership consultants overshadowing the genuine development of authentic leaders. He noted that numerous leadership programs often favor temporary solutions rather than addressing the fundamental problems of leadership shortfalls. In his book, Vetri aims to underscore vital attributes that today's leaders commonly overlook or miss, offering a resource for self-reflection and deep understanding.

Vetri has guided and mentored many senior leaders, catalyzing profound behavior and habit transformations. His notable contributions include authoring the first edition of "Spiritual Leadership".

Through this book, Vetri aims to inspire the leaders to modify their behavior and habit, transform their personal culture and concentrate on their inner development. By doing so, leaders can positively impact employee engagement reduce the need for firefighting and free up more time strategic activities.

Outside of his professional life, Vetri finds pleasure in exploring ancient spiritual sites, interacting with diverse individuals, and engaging in meaningful conversations about life purpose. These passions not only enhance his personal experiences but also shape his approach to leadership coaching.

Vetri Lives by the guiding philosophy that no matter how proficient he becomes, there is always someone somewhere who is better. This belief keeps his ego in check and drives continual and humanity.